GCSE English

The Crucible

by Arthur Miller

Studying English texts can give you a real headache,
but happily this CGP book makes your life just a little bit easier.

This book has everything you need to write a brilliant essay about *The Crucible*.
It doesn't just tell you what happens — it's got analysis of the main characters,
themes, historical background and language features too.

Plus, there are plenty of practice questions and a worked exam answer
with tips on how to improve your grade on the big day.

And of course, we've done our best to make the whole
experience at least vaguely entertaining for you.

The Text Guide

CONTENTS

Introduction

Section One — Background and Context

Section Two — Discussion of Acts

Section Three — Characters

CONTENTS

Section Four — Themes

Section Five — Writer's Techniques

Section Six — Exam Advice

Published by CGP

Editors:
Claire Boulter
Catherine Heygate
Rachael Powers
Holly Poynton

Contributors:
Samantha Bensted
Marian Feeley

With thanks to Luke von Kotze and Elisabeth Sanderson for the proofreading.

Acknowledgements:
Cover Illustration by David DeFigueredo © 2011
Images on pages 3, 4, 12, 13, 23, 24, 27, 28, 29, 31, 36, 37, 39, 40, 43, 44 & 46 © AJ Chan
With thanks to The Kobal Collection for permission to use the images on pages 1, 3, 14, 15, 26 & 45
With thanks to Rex Features for permission to use the images on pages 3, 5, 17, 22, 32, 38, 47 & 48
With thanks to Daniella Zalcman for permission to use the image on page 3
With thanks to iStockphoto.com for permission to use the images on pages 2, 6 & 7
With thanks to Getty Images for permission to use the images on pages 8 & 9
Image on page 1: On Trial, when Satan came to Salem, 1978 (gouache on paper) by English School, (20th century) Private Collection/ © Look and Learn/ The Bridgeman Art Library
Image on page 5: Examination of a Witch, 1853 (oil on canvas) by Matteson, Tompkins Harrison (1813-84) © Peabody Essex Museum, Salem, Massachusetts, USA/ The Bridgeman Art Library
Images on pages 5, 18, 19, 25, 49 & 50 from the Oxford Theatre Guild's production at Oxford Playhouse in March/April 2009. © Felicity Peacock
Image on page 9 from the comic book 'Is This Tomorrow' published in 1947 by the Catechetical Guild Educational Society of St. Paul, Minnesota. Reproduced under the terms of the Creative Commons Licence http://creativecommons.org/licenses/by/3.0/
With thanks to Alamy for permission to use the images on pages 16 & 33
With thanks to The Moviestore Collection for permission to use the image on page 30

Every effort has been made to locate copyright holders and obtain permission to reproduce sources. For those sources where it has been difficult to trace the originator of the work, we would be grateful for information. If any copyright holder would like us to make an amendment to the acknowledgements, please notify us and we will gladly update the book at the next reprint. Thank you.

ISBN: 978 1 84762 666 0
Printed by Elanders Ltd, Newcastle upon Tyne.
Clipart from Corel®

Based on the classic CGP style created by Richard Parsons.

Introduction to 'The Crucible' and Arthur Miller

The Crucible is about witch-hunts

- *The Crucible* is a play about <u>witch trials</u> in <u>Salem Village</u> in the American state of Massachusetts in <u>1692</u>.

- It's based on <u>real events</u> and <u>real people</u>, but it's a <u>fictional</u> account of what happened.

What really happened in 1692

1) In February 1692, several girls in Salem started having <u>fits</u> and <u>accused</u> other villagers of <u>bewitching</u> them.

2) Over the next eight months, <u>over 150 people</u> were <u>arrested</u> for witchcraft. Nineteen of them were <u>hanged</u>.

Arthur Miller experienced a 1950s 'witch-hunt'

- In the 1950s, the House Un-American Activities Committee (HUAC), a body set up to investigate radical political groups, accused thousands of people of being <u>communists</u>. The people accused were <u>aggressively questioned</u>, and many <u>lost their jobs</u> or were <u>imprisoned</u> with <u>no evidence</u>.

- Miller wrote *The Crucible* to highlight the danger of modern-day '<u>witch-hunts</u>' like these.

1915	Born in New York.
1936	Wrote his <u>first play</u>, 'No Villain'.
1952	Miller's friend Elia Kazan was questioned about communist activity by the <u>House Un-American Activities Committee</u> (HUAC). Kazan's experience inspired Miller to write '<u>The Crucible</u>'.
1953	'The Crucible' opened on Broadway.
1956	Married <u>Marilyn Monroe</u>
1957	Miller was questioned by HUAC. He was <u>sentenced</u> to thirty days in prison and wasn't allowed a <u>passport</u>. He was also <u>blacklisted</u> — he wasn't allowed to <u>work</u>.
1958	Miller's <u>conviction</u> was <u>overturned</u>.
2005	Died, aged 89.

© THE KOBAL COLLECTION

Background Information

Salem was a small village in Massachusetts

In 1692 Salem was a <u>small</u> village of about 150 houses.   Here are the <u>key locations</u> in the play:

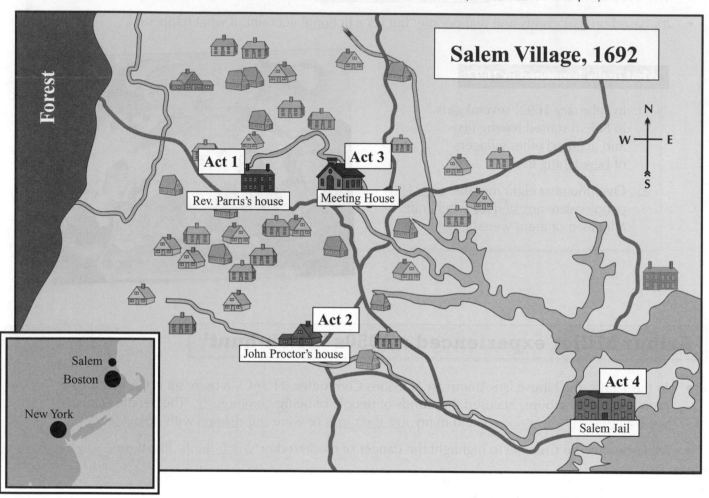

Life in Salem was tough

- The people of Salem were <u>Puritans</u> (a strict religious group) — they spent most of their time <u>working</u> or <u>praying</u>.

- It was <u>difficult</u> to grow enough food to eat, and they were sometimes <u>attacked</u> by Native Americans.

- Problems like illness were often seen as the <u>Devil's work</u>.

- People convicted of <u>witchcraft</u> or <u>Devil worship</u> were often <u>executed</u> to protect the village.

Who's Who in Salem

John Proctor...

...is a well-respected local farmer. He had an affair with Abigail, which he still feels guilty about.

Elizabeth Proctor...

...is John's wife. She's still loyal to him despite the affair, but she can't forget about it.

Reverend Parris...

...is the minister of Salem. He's more worried about money and his career than about God.

Abigail Williams...

...is Parris's niece. She's still in love with John — and she's prepared to do anything to win him back.

Reverend Hale...

...is a witchcraft expert who's called in to examine the girls.

Mary Warren...

...is a shy girl who works for the Proctors. She's friends with Abigail.

Deputy-Governor Danforth...

...is the judge in charge of the witchcraft trials. He's obsessed with his job and reputation.

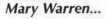

The Putnams...

...are a local couple who own a lot of land. They think other people are out to get them.

Rebecca Nurse...

...is a local farmer's wife. She's known for her goodness and courage.

Giles Corey...

...is a local farmer who's had arguments with the Putnams over land. He's not afraid to speak his mind.

'The Crucible' — Plot Summary

'The Crucible'... what happens when?

Here's a little recap of the main events of *The Crucible*. It's a good idea to learn what happens when, so that you know exactly how the plot progresses and how all the important events fit together.

Act One — Reverend Parris's house, spring 1692

- Reverend Parris caught his daughter Betty and niece Abigail dancing with his slave Tituba and some of the other village girls. Now Betty is ill. Parris accuses Abigail of conjuring spirits.

- Abigail threatens to hurt the girls if they tell anyone that she drank a potion to kill John Proctor's wife, Elizabeth.

- John Proctor comes in. He had an affair with Abigail when she was his servant, but it's over. Abigail tells him Betty's illness isn't caused by witchcraft.

- Reverend Hale, a witchcraft 'expert', arrives.

- Abigail accuses Tituba of summoning the devil. Tituba confesses and starts accusing others.

- Abigail and Betty claim to have seen people with the Devil.

Act Two — the Proctors' house, a week later

- The witchcraft trials have started. Elizabeth believes that John can stop the trials by telling the court that Abigail is lying, but John is reluctant.

- The Proctors' servant, Mary Warren, returns from Salem — thirty-nine women are in jail for witchcraft. Elizabeth's name has been mentioned in court. Mary gives Elizabeth a doll she's made.

- Reverend Hale arrives to question Elizabeth.

- Giles Corey and Francis Nurse burst in — their wives have been arrested.

- Two court officials arrest Elizabeth — Abigail claims Elizabeth's spirit stuck a needle in her.

- John tells Mary she must tell the court that Abigail is lying.

Act Three — the courtroom

- John Proctor takes Mary Warren to tell the judges that the girls are <u>lying</u>.

- Danforth, the main judge, tells John that Elizabeth is <u>pregnant</u> and <u>won't</u> be hanged.

- Lots of villagers have signed a <u>testimony</u> to say that Elizabeth, Martha Corey and Rebecca Nurse aren't witches. Danforth orders everyone who signed it to be arrested.

- Mary tells the court the girls are <u>pretending</u> to be bewitched. They start pretending that Mary has bewitched them.

© Felicity Peacock

- John admits to his <u>affair</u> with Abigail to <u>ruin</u> her <u>reputation</u>. Elizabeth's brought in and asked if it's true. She <u>denies</u> it, which destroys John's case against Abigail.

- The girls pretend that Mary's spirit is <u>attacking</u> them. She breaks down and <u>accuses John</u> of doing the Devil's work. John is <u>arrested</u>.

Act Four — Salem jail, autumn 1692

- Hale and Parris are persuading the prisoners to <u>confess</u>. Abigail has <u>robbed</u> Parris and <u>vanished</u>.

- The judges ask Elizabeth to <u>persuade</u> John to <u>confess</u>. She agrees to speak to him, but she <u>won't</u> promise to try to persuade him.

© 20thC.Fox/Everett/Rex Features

- Over a <u>hundred</u> people have confessed. <u>Giles Corey</u> wouldn't plead guilty or not guilty, so he was <u>tortured</u> to death.

- John confesses, but he <u>refuses</u> to say he's seen <u>other prisoners</u> with the devil.

- John tears up his confession. He's led out to be <u>hanged</u>.

- Parris and Hale ask Elizabeth to persuade John to confess again, but she <u>refuses</u>.

Think that's the end of this book? That's witchful thinking...

So... *The Crucible* is a fictional play based on real events in the 17th century, but it also relates to events in the 20th century. If all that makes perfect sense, reward yourself with a gold star and a cuppa, and move on to Section One. If you're still a bit hazy on the plot, or just want a break from revision, check out the cartoon at the back of the book.

What Life was Like in Salem, Massachusetts in 1692

Back in 1692, Salem was a hard-working, God-fearing society full of hope for the future.
Today it brings to mind witch trials, horror films and Sabrina's cat. Time for a re-brand, maybe.

Settlers in Salem were Puritans

1) A group of English settlers came to America in 1626 and founded a settlement in Massachusetts. The settlement was named Salem in 1629.

2) These first settlers were Puritans — Christians who followed the teachings of the Bible extremely strictly.

3) The Puritans had broken away from the Church of England because they thought it was too tolerant of people who didn't follow God's word exactly. They believed:

- in hell and the Devil. They feared God and what would happen if they sinned.

- that entertainment led to sin — games, dancing and even Christmas were all banned.

- that they were superior to the Native Americans who they thought were 'heathens'. They were intolerant of all beliefs other than their own.

A heathen is someone who doesn't believe in God.

Salem society was a theocracy

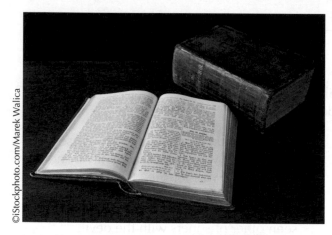

©iStockphoto.com/Marek Walica

1) A theocracy is a society ruled by people who are considered to be guided by God. Laws in a theocracy are based on the religious laws in the Bible.

2) The Puritans believed that community was important. Miller says that the function of the theocracy was "to keep the community together".

3) The people in charge in Salem thought it was their responsibility to make people confess their sins, turn their back on the Devil and rejoin the church.

Miller uses symbolism to emphasise the burden of theocracy throughout *The Crucible* (see page 49).

Puritan women and children had a raw deal

1) Puritan children were seen as young adults. They were expected to go to church and work hard.

2) They didn't get the chance to play and had few toys. They had to be well behaved and avoid emotional outbursts.

3) Children were punished if they behaved badly.

Women were associated with sin and temptation in Puritan society because of the biblical story of Adam and Eve. God banished Adam and Eve from the Garden of Eden after Eve tempted Adam to eat fruit from the forbidden tree.

4) Women were seen as socially inferior — they had less power and fewer choices than men.

What Life was Like in Salem, Massachusetts in 1692

Many Puritans believed the Devil was out to get them

1) Life was tough for the Puritans — there were outbreaks of <u>smallpox</u>, <u>attacks</u> from Native Americans and their crops often <u>didn't grow</u>.

2) When unexplained things happened in the community, people often thought that it was the <u>Devil's work</u> or that they had been <u>cursed</u>.

3) Some people thought that witches worked for the Devil — so accusing someone of witchcraft meant accusing them of being <u>unchristian</u>.

> **Theme — Envy and Revenge**
>
> In *The Crucible* Ann Putnam <u>wants</u> to <u>blame</u> someone for the deaths of her seven children — she accuses Rebecca Nurse of witchcraft as a way of <u>making sense</u> of her own <u>anger</u> and <u>grief</u>.

The Crucible is based on the real Salem witch trials

© iStockphoto.com/jean-luc stadler

1) In 1692 Abigail Williams and Betty Parris claimed to be <u>victims</u> of witchcraft. They <u>accused</u> three Salem women of being <u>witches</u>.

2) It was <u>easy</u> for the people of Salem to believe these three women were witches because they were <u>different</u>. Sarah Good was a beggar, Sarah Osburn didn't go to <u>church</u> and Tituba was a <u>black slave</u>.

3) The trials led to <u>mass hysteria</u> and over 150 people were accused of witchcraft. Some accusers saw the trials as an easy way of getting their hands on the <u>land</u> and <u>property</u> of <u>ruined</u> women.

4) Some of the accused <u>confessed</u> to being <u>guilty</u> of witchcraft — it was the only way to <u>avoid</u> being sentenced to <u>death</u>. It was almost <u>impossible</u> to prove yourself <u>innocent</u> once you'd been accused.

5) Those who refused to confess were <u>killed</u>. Altogether 26 people were tried and <u>all</u> of them were found <u>guilty</u>. 19 of them were hanged.

But Miller changed some things for *The Crucible*

Arthur Miller based *The Crucible* on <u>real people</u> and <u>events</u> but altered some parts of the story to make it more <u>dramatic</u>. For example:

- Abigail is <u>older</u> in *The Crucible* (she's 17 rather than 12), and has an <u>affair</u> with Proctor. This gives Abigail a <u>motive</u> for accusing his wife, Elizabeth, of witchcraft. It also makes her actions more <u>shocking</u> because she's older and should know <u>better</u>.

- He cut out large sections of the court proceedings to avoid lengthy, boring court scenes. The audience only sees the <u>dramatic</u> bits.

Remember that the characters are Puritans...

The historical background on these pages gives you an insight into the religious world the characters live in. It helps to explain why they act the way they do, so it's worth mentioning it in your exam.

Section One — Background and Context

The USA and Communism in the 1950s

"What do witch trials 300 years ago have in common with the political climate in the 1950s?" you may ask. Well Miller saw loads of similarities between the persecution in Salem and the persecution of communists.

The USA is a capitalist country...

1) Capitalism is a way of life which encourages people to <u>work hard</u> to earn <u>money</u> for <u>themselves</u>.

2) In capitalist countries, most businesses are <u>privately owned</u> — the owners get to keep most of the <u>profits</u> for themselves rather than giving them to the <u>government</u>. The government also tries not to <u>interfere</u> too much with the way businesses are <u>run</u>.

3) In the 1950s, Western countries like the <u>UK</u> and <u>USA</u> hoped that <u>capitalism</u> would encourage <u>recovery</u> after World War II.

... and in the 1950s it was afraid of communist Russia

1) Communism is the <u>opposite</u> of capitalism. A communist society is one where everyone is <u>equal</u> (at least in theory) and there's no such thing as <u>private ownership</u>.

2) In the 1950s, some <u>powerful</u> countries like <u>China</u> and the <u>USSR</u> (which included modern day Russia) were communist.

> Much like the characters of *The Crucible* feared witchcraft, Americans feared the threat of the <u>USSR</u> and <u>communism</u>.

3) Americans were <u>afraid</u> that communist countries, particularly the <u>USSR</u>, were trying to <u>take over the world</u>.

Tension between the two countries led to the Cold War

1) The Cold War wasn't really a <u>war</u> — it's the name given to the period of <u>political</u>, <u>military</u> and <u>economic rivalry</u> between the USSR and the USA (and their allies) after the Second World War.

2) The two countries were in competition — they both wanted to become the strongest <u>superpower</u>.

3) Both sides had <u>nuclear weapons</u>. They were afraid that the other side would attack and cause <u>massive devastation</u>.

4) Some Americans thought that <u>communism</u> might spread to the USA and <u>threaten capitalism</u> and their political <u>values</u>.

> Slogans like 'reds under the bed' warned Americans that communists were lurking everywhere ready to <u>attack</u> — <u>propaganda</u> helped to feed the flames of hysteria.

'Superpower' is the name given to a rich and powerful country that's capable of influencing other countries.

The USA and Communism in the 1950s

Is this fear of the unknown starting to sound a bit familiar? I should hope so. Don't fall into the trap of bypassing the historical context — it's absolutely crucial to understanding the play's message.

McCarthyism was a real-life 'witch hunt'

1) McCarthyism gets its name from the man who started it, Senator Joe McCarthy.

2) During the 1950s, McCarthy campaigned against communism — he claimed that there were communists in the US government.

3) He hunted communists and was supported by lots of influential politicians. He was famous for aggressive interrogation and making accusations with little evidence.

4) Many of the people who were accused lost their jobs or were imprisoned.

5) If you were arrested, you were encouraged to accuse friends and colleagues to clear your name — this made people paranoid.

6) These proceedings were labelled 'witch hunts' because people were accused of crimes and punished with little or no evidence.

> Naming someone as a communist could ruin their reputation, so it was used by some as a way of getting revenge. This is similar to how some characters in *The Crucible* use the witch trials to get revenge.

The persecution of Miller's friends shaped *The Crucible*

1) Arthur Miller wrote *The Crucible* in 1953 during the Cold War and McCarthy's anti-communist campaign.

2) Many writers and entertainers were accused of communism, including Miller's friend Elia Kazan.

3) Miller himself was also accused. He refused to name any of his colleagues as communists, and as a result he was fined and had his passport confiscated.

4) The hysteria about communism during the McCarthy era is similar to the hysteria about witchcraft that Miller wrote about in *The Crucible* — people were paranoid.

5) Like the trials in the play, people could be arrested with very little evidence and it was very difficult to prove you were innocent once you had been accused.

A group of communists are taken to jail following their trial.

© AFP/Getty Images

KEY QUOTE

"It's hard proof, hard as a rock, the judges said."

And we know that the judges were right... oh wait. The flimsy evidence used to convict witches in Salem mirrors the way communists in 1950s America were accused and even punished without reliable evidence.

Practice Questions

Here's a quick warm-up to the main event and a chance to see how much knowledge you've absorbed. If you can fire through these bad boys without a problem, move on to the in-depth questions over the page. If these questions prove a bit tricky, read through the section again and have another go.

Quick Questions

1) Why did the Puritans break away from the Church of England?

2) Give examples of two things expected of Puritan children.

3) Who were the first three women in Salem to be accused of witchcraft?

4) Why might these women have been considered 'different'?

5) How many people were accused of witchcraft during the Salem witch trials?

6) What did some people have to gain by accusing women of witchcraft?

7) What are the major differences between communist and capitalist societies?

8) Briefly explain what the Cold War was.

9) Give two reasons why America was afraid of the USSR during the 1950s.

10) Who was Joe McCarthy?

Practice Questions

Welcome to the in-depth questions, a lovely selection of questions which are perfect pre-exam revision. Aim to write a couple of paragraphs per question and remember to back up your points with examples. Revisit them the night before the exam to refresh your memory of all the key events and the historical significance of the play.

In-depth Questions

1) How might Miller's own experiences be said to have influenced his writing in *The Crucible*?

2) How might the way children were treated in Puritan society have influenced the way that they behave in *The Crucible*?

3) Which parts of the real Salem witch trials did Miller change for *The Crucible* and why?

4) In what ways do you think *The Crucible* was influenced by the historical context in which it was written?

5) How were the accusations of witchcraft in Salem in the 1690s similar to the accusations of communism in America in the 1950s?

Analysis of Act One — Parris's House

Here's some analysis of the important bits, starting conveniently with Act One. It probably won't make much sense if the play isn't fresh in your mind, so either reread it or have it open next to you while you read this...

Parris is worried about his reputation

1) Act One opens with Reverend Parris *"evidently in prayer"* at his daughter's bedside — the word <u>evidently</u> suggests that when Parris prays he wants it to be obvious that he's praying. <u>Appearances</u> are very important to him.

2) It's also clear that Parris is more bothered about his <u>reputation</u> than the welfare of his <u>daughter</u> — "my ministry's at stake, my ministry and perhaps your cousin's life".

3) There's already <u>hysteria</u> about the rumours of witchcraft — Parris's parlour "is packed with people". This shows that everyone's <u>involved</u> in everyone else's <u>business</u>.

Stage directions

Spring <u>sunlight</u> streams through the window. The light <u>contrasts</u> with the <u>dark</u>, <u>oppressive</u> events. For more on the symbolism of light see p.48 and 50.

Theme — Fear

Parris <u>denies</u> that witchcraft is responsible for Betty's illness — it wouldn't look good if his daughter and niece were mixed up in black magic. But he's <u>scared</u> that if he's not seen to be taking witchcraft seriously, he'll <u>lose his authority</u>.

We're introduced to Abigail and see her true colours

KEY EVENT

1) Parris asks Abigail about her <u>reputation</u> — he's heard <u>rumours</u> she's "soiled" — which suggests that she's not a virgin. Abigail seems to be someone who likes to <u>break the rules</u>.

2) Abigail <u>denies</u> she's done anything wrong, but it turns out she's had an affair with John Proctor — she's a <u>liar</u>. She's also <u>ruthless</u> and <u>vindictive</u> — she wants to <u>kill</u> John Proctor's wife Elizabeth.

3) Abigail's <u>tone of voice</u> and <u>actions</u> reveal a lot about her. For example, she *"lowers her eyes"* and talks *"innocently"* to Parris, but when John Proctor comes in she talks *"tauntingly"*. This shows that she's a <u>good actor</u>, and that she can <u>change</u> her behaviour depending on who she's with (see page 26).

© AJ Chan

Theme — Envy and Revenge

<u>Envy</u> and <u>revenge</u> are the driving forces behind most of Abigail's actions.

4) Abigail is <u>perceptive</u> — for example she knows that John Proctor has been looking up at her window. This shows she's <u>skilful</u> at reading people — which she uses to her <u>advantage</u> when she makes <u>accusations</u>.

Analysis of Act One — Parris's House

There's already tension in Salem

1) The people of Salem see themselves as a <u>strong</u>, <u>united</u> community but it doesn't take much to <u>divide</u> them.

2) Parris tells Proctor "There is a party in this church. I am not blind; there is a faction and a party." He's <u>paranoid</u> that people are plotting to <u>get rid</u> of him.

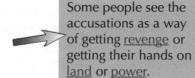

Some people see the accusations as a way of getting <u>revenge</u> or getting their hands on <u>land</u> or <u>power</u>.

3) Act One introduces the <u>motives</u> for the later accusations:

- <u>Ann Putnam</u> is jealous of <u>Rebecca</u>, because all of Rebecca's children survived, but most of Ann's died.
- <u>Parris</u> thinks that he should be <u>paid more</u> and describes himself as "persecuted" in Salem.
- <u>Giles Corey</u> is unpopular because he often <u>takes people to court</u> for real or imagined insults.
- There are disagreements over <u>land</u> — e.g. Putnam and Proctor both think they own the same bit of forest.

Reverend Hale arrives and the accusations begin

1) <u>Lies</u> are already circulating — Mr Collins claims he saw Betty flying. Nobody knows what's <u>true</u> and what's <u>not</u> — this contributes to the growing sense of <u>hysteria</u>.

2) When Parris accuses Abigail of witchcraft she's sure "Betty's not witched", but when Hale accuses her of witchcraft she quickly <u>changes</u> her story and <u>blames</u> Tituba — she's an easy <u>scapegoat</u>.

A scapegoat is someone who is singled out and punished for something they haven't done

3) Tituba initially <u>denies</u> witchcraft, but quickly sees that she'll be hanged unless she <u>confesses</u> and <u>names other people</u> — she can't win.

© AJ Chan

4) When Tituba confesses to seeing the Devil, Putnam seizes the opportunity to <u>influence</u> her — he asks "Did you ever see Sarah Good with him?". By mentioning Sarah Good's name, Putnam <u>encourages</u> Tituba to accuse her — this is called the <u>power of suggestion</u>.

5) Abigail confesses too so that she can <u>accuse</u> other villagers, especially the women who <u>gossiped</u> about her. She exploits her power to get <u>revenge</u>.

6) Act One ends with the girls <u>accusing</u> people with *"great glee"* and *"ecstatic cries"* — it's <u>creepy</u> how much they're <u>enjoying</u> it.

Write about how Miller builds a sense of hysteria...

Don't forget to say that rumours and accusations are flying around from the start — this builds tension and hysteria. The accusations snowball, and before you know it half of Salem is apparently pals with the Devil.

Analysis of Act Two — The Proctors' House

Act Two opens in the Proctors' house. A week has passed since the girls first started making accusations, and everything's getting out of control.

Proctor and Elizabeth's relationship is strained

1) Their relationship is <u>cold</u> and <u>lacks passion</u> — Elizabeth "receives" Proctor's kiss, and Proctor complains "It's winter in here yet". The lack of <u>warmth</u> and <u>joy</u> in the house reflects the problems with their <u>relationship</u>.

Stage directions

The Proctors' house is "low" and "dark", which gives a feeling of being <u>trapped</u>. But there's a door which opens on to <u>fields</u>, which gives a sense of <u>hope</u> for the Proctors' <u>relationship</u>. For more on the setting see p.43.

Theme — Loyalty

<u>Contrast</u> this with Proctor and Elizabeth's relationship in Act Four — it's <u>ironic</u> that Abigail's attempts to break up their marriage bring them <u>closer</u> together.

2) They're <u>not honest</u> with each other either — Elizabeth "would speak but cannot", and Proctor lies about seeing Abigail alone. This lack of openness could <u>symbolise</u> the <u>lies</u> and <u>secrecy</u> within Salem.

Mary comes back from court

KEY EVENT

1) Mary tells the Proctors that she's <u>sick</u> — her <u>conscience</u> is finally starting to catch up with her.

2) She believes that sending women to their deaths is "God's work" — this shows how <u>flawed</u> theocracy is. The court would rather hang women than listen to <u>reason</u> and admit they've been misled.

3) Her behaviour is <u>erratic</u>. When she enters the room she is acting with "*strangeness*". She breaks down and "*sobs*" and then stands up for herself with a "*stamp of her foot*". This reminds the audience how <u>young</u> she is.

The girls have been given power

1) The girls are <u>young</u> and <u>unmarried</u> — they're usually at the bottom of the social ladder in Salem. They're relishing their new-found <u>power</u>.

For more on <u>religious language</u> have a look at p.46.

2) People now "part like the sea for Israel" for Abigail. This shows the <u>authority</u> she's gained.

3) It's not just Abigail who has gained <u>confidence</u> — Mary talks to Proctor with "*impatience*".

4) Even though lots of the women who are accused have <u>good reputations</u>, the judges <u>believe</u> the girls without question — they can't accept that <u>children</u> are capable of committing <u>sin</u>.

© 20TH CENTURY FOX / THE KOBAL COLLECTION

Analysis of Act Two — The Proctors' House

Proctor wrestles with his conscience

1) Elizabeth <u>urges</u> Proctor to tell the court that the girls are lying but he's <u>reluctant</u>. He's worried his affair with Abigail will be discovered — his <u>reputation</u> is more important to him than his <u>conscience</u> at this point.

Theme — Conscience

If Proctor had told the court the truth when Elizabeth asked him to, he might have been able to <u>prevent</u> the witch trials getting so <u>out of hand</u>. He realises this later, and the <u>guilt</u> drives his attempt to <u>overthrow</u> the court.

© 20TH CENTURY FOX / THE KOBAL COLLECTION

Theme — Religious intolerance

Knowing the Bible <u>inside out</u> was <u>crucial</u> to being a good Christian in Puritan Salem. Some characters in *The Crucible* <u>doubt</u> whether Proctor and Elizabeth are good Christians because they haven't had their third child <u>baptised</u>, don't go to <u>church</u> often and John <u>can't</u> <u>remember</u> all the Commandments.

2) Hale comes to the Proctors' house — he's visiting all the families whose names came up in court. He asks the Proctors' to recite the <u>Ten Commandments</u> to test how Christian they are.

3) Proctor forgets the commandment about <u>adultery</u> — this is <u>ironic</u>, as it's the sin he's most <u>guilty</u> of because of his affair with Abigail. It also makes Hale <u>suspicious</u> — revealing the link between Proctor's <u>infidelity</u> and his <u>downfall</u>.

Things are getting out of control

1) Hale goes to the Proctors' house <u>without</u> the court's authority — this shows he's losing <u>faith</u> in the court system.

2) He feels like things are out of control when <u>respectable</u> women like Elizabeth and Rebecca are arrested — "if Rebecca Nurse be tainted, then nothing's left to stop the whole green world from burning". He's realised that not all these women can be <u>guilty</u>.

Proctor <u>won't</u> sacrifice his reputation to save women like Goody Osburn — it's only when Elizabeth is accused that he acts. This is another <u>flaw</u> in his character.

3) Hale can't <u>stop</u> the accusations though because he'd be admitting that the other women sentenced were <u>innocent</u> too.

4) Proctor realises that he must <u>expose</u> Abigail now that Elizabeth's been accused. He's given <u>courage</u> by the fact that Mary already knows about his <u>affair</u> — it shows him it's not quite as <u>secret</u> as he thought.

Comment on the significance of Hale's visit...

Although this act is set in the Proctors' home, Hale brings the trial to them. You'll impress the examiner if you mention that the couple can't escape the shocking accusations which are spiralling out of control.

Analysis of Act Three — The Courtroom

Two judges, Hathorne and Danforth, have arrived to carry out the trials.
It's not so much 'good cop, bad cop' as 'bad cop, even worse cop'.

Danforth is determined to find witches

Challenging the court is extremely dangerous. The court sees itself as doing God's work, so undermining the court is an attack on God — this shows the men's bravery in trying to save their wives.

1) At the start of Act Three the audience can only hear voices from offstage — this represents how ordinary people are excluded from what happens in the court and can't influence the decisions the court makes.

2) Giles Corey and Francis Nurse have evidence to prove their wives are innocent, but Danforth and the other judges are reluctant to accept evidence which contradicts the court. The judges see an attack on the court as an attack on themselves.

3) Proctor gives the judges a testimony signed by ninety-one people which confirms that Martha, Rebecca and Elizabeth are good women. Danforth orders that everyone who signed it be arrested.

4) The testimony represents Salem's moral values — they're a community and people unite to help their neighbours. When Danforth arrests the people who signed the testimony it shows how the trials are tearing the society of Salem apart.

© Photos 12 / Alamy

5) Parris suggests that Proctor and Giles are trying to overthrow the court. He's trying to discredit them because he's terrified that his daughter and niece will be exposed as frauds.

Stage directions

The sunlight pouring through the windows symbolises the light that the court hopes to shine on those accused, but is also ironic, because the court doesn't uncover the truth.

The language reveals a lot about power

The way the characters speak to each other in this act is very important.
For more about the use of language elsewhere in the play see p.46-47.

- Nearly everything Parris says in this act ends with an exclamation mark — this shows his growing fear that his position in society might be threatened.

- Hale doesn't say much in this act — he's resigned to the fact that people are being accused and there's nothing he can do to stop it. When he does speak he's often interrupted. This shows that Hale's less powerful than the other court officials.

- By this point, Abigail is one of the most powerful characters and her language reflects this. She says in an *"open threat"* to Danforth: "Think you to be so mighty that the power of Hell may not turn *your* wits?" She's so confident of herself she's intimidating the judges.

Analysis of Act Three — The Courtroom

Proctor reaches a turning point

1) Proctor tries to <u>stop</u> the trials but his attempts are <u>useless</u>. Although 91 people have signed the testimony Danforth sees it as <u>worthless</u>. It's ironic that their signatures have <u>no impact</u> on the trial at all while his is <u>powerful</u> enough to send 72 people to their <u>deaths</u>.

2) Danforth's surprised to see Francis Nurse "in such uproar" even though his wife has been sentenced to <u>death</u>. Danforth doesn't expect the men to show <u>emotion</u> — he's <u>inhumane</u>.

3) As a last resort, Proctor admits to his affair. If he can prove that Abigail <u>isn't pure</u>, then she <u>can't</u> be channelling the voice of God, and therefore must be <u>lying</u>.

> Admitting to the affair shows that Proctor is finally ready to deal with the <u>consequences</u> of his <u>sins</u>.

4) Elizabeth is called to confirm whether Abigail and Proctor had an affair. She says they didn't — she's lying to protect Proctor's <u>reputation</u>, but ends up <u>condemning</u> him instead.

> Elizabeth is described as someone who "<u>cannot</u> lie" — she thinks lying is a sin. But she lies to save Proctor's <u>reputation</u>, showing how <u>loyal</u> she is to him.

Mary can't win

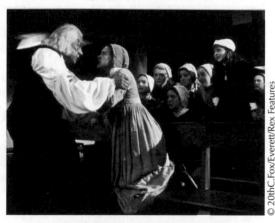

1) All the evidence against the girls has been <u>disproved</u>, and the judges threaten Mary with <u>jail</u> and <u>hanging</u> if she won't admit that she's telling <u>lies</u> about never having seen the Devil.

2) It's clear that the judges are <u>biased</u> in favour of the girls — they're worried that their <u>reputations</u> will be damaged if they admit they've been <u>deceived</u> by a group of young girls and sent <u>innocent</u> people to their <u>deaths</u>.

3) As soon as Hale <u>turns on</u> Abigail, she pretends that Mary's <u>spirit</u> is attacking her in the form of a <u>yellow bird</u>. The bird is <u>invisible</u> to everyone but the girls — this shows how easily the court will accept evidence they can't actually <u>see</u>.

> For more on the <u>symbolism</u> of <u>birds</u> have a look at p.49.

© 20thC.Fox/Everett/Rex Features

Miller uses the symbolism of fire to represent the court

1) Miller uses lots of <u>imagery</u> of <u>fire</u> in Act Three.

2) For example, <u>Danforth</u> refers to the court as a "hot fire" that "melts down all concealment".

3) At the end of the act, <u>John Proctor</u> compares the court to the <u>fires of Hell</u>.

4) The fact that <u>different characters</u> use the <u>same imagery</u> in different ways shows how the <u>court</u> and <u>theocracy</u> has <u>divided</u> Salem. For more on symbolism in *The Crucible*, see p.48-49.

KEY QUOTE

"since I come to Salem this man is blackening my name."

Some people never change... Even after everything that's happened, Parris is still obsessed with his reputation. Meanwhile, other characters — like Proctor and Hale — go on real journeys over the course of the play.

Section Two — Discussion of Acts

Analysis of Act Four — The Jail

Act Four is set in Salem jail, where the prisoners are waiting to be hanged.
In this act John Proctor finally has to decide whether to confess or not...

Salem is falling apart

1) Months have passed and Salem is <u>crumbling</u>.
   Cows are roaming the village because their owners are
   in <u>jail</u> or <u>dead</u>, <u>orphans</u> are wandering in the streets and
   the crops are <u>rotting</u>. Salem has become a <u>hellish</u> place.

Stage directions

The jail is <u>dark</u> and <u>dirty</u>, symbolising how events in Salem are driven by <u>malice</u>.

2) Witchcraft trials are also taking place in the nearby town of <u>Andover</u> but there are rumours the
   people there have <u>overthrown</u> the courts — this suggests that the same thing may happen in Salem.

3) Tituba mistakes the bellowing of a <u>cow</u> for the call of the <u>Devil</u> — this suggests that she's been
   driven <u>insane</u> by her <u>imprisonment</u>. It could also represent the <u>madness</u> of the <u>whole situation</u>.

Parris is having doubts

1) Parris is showing signs of being <u>mentally unstable</u> —
   Hathorne describes him as having a "mad look".

2) Abigail has robbed him and <u>vanished</u> — Parris
   waits two days before telling the court she's missing
   — he's afraid to face up to reality.

Now Abigail's missing, Danforth wants a <u>confession</u> from one of the prisoners to <u>justify</u> hanging the others and make it look like he's doing the <u>right thing</u>.

At this point in the play, <u>Parris</u> has realised that the court has <u>gone too far</u>. His main concern is <u>his own safety</u> — he wants to <u>postpone</u> the hangings not because he wants to <u>save</u> Rebecca or Proctor but because he's afraid of <u>riots</u>.

3) He wants to <u>postpone</u> the hangings but
   the judges refuse — they think any sign of
   <u>uncertainty</u> would damage their <u>reputations</u>.

Hale is trying to save the prisoners' lives

1) Hale has a <u>guilty conscience</u> — he
   describes himself as Proctor's "murderer".

2) Hale refers to the girls' accusations as "the
   harlots' cry". This shows how <u>opinions</u> of
   the girls have <u>changed</u> — before they were
   seen as <u>saints</u>, now they're seen as <u>sinners</u>.

3) He's trying to <u>make amends</u> for his part in
   the witch-hunts by persuading the prisoners
   to confess. He knows that the confessions
   are <u>lies</u>, but he'd rather save <u>lives</u> than <u>souls</u>.

© Felicity Peacock

Analysis of Act Four — The Jail

Elizabeth won't tell Proctor whether or not he should confess

© Felicity Peacock

1) Elizabeth has been summoned to try to <u>convince</u> Proctor to confess. She doesn't want him to <u>damn himself</u> by <u>lying</u> — but she doesn't want him to <u>die</u> either.

2) Proctor is torn between <u>confessing</u> and <u>living</u> with the guilt of making it seem that the <u>other prisoners</u> are guilty of witchcraft too, or dying a <u>dignified death</u>.

3) He believes he's <u>already damned</u> for committing adultery, so the extra sin of making a false confession won't matter. He doesn't want to be hanged "like a saint" — he sees <u>goodness</u> in people like Rebecca, but <u>not</u> in himself.

4) Proctor wants Elizabeth to <u>forgive</u> him, but she <u>refuses</u>. She thinks <u>her</u> forgiveness isn't important — it's more important that he <u>forgives himself</u>. She confesses that his affair was partly <u>her fault</u> to make him see that he's a good man.

Proctor confesses, but then withdraws his confession

KEY EVENT

1) Hale and Parris are keen for Danforth to accept Proctor's confession — Hale because he knows that Proctor is <u>innocent</u>, and Parris because he <u>fears</u> for his own life.

2) When Proctor confesses and says he didn't see anyone with the Devil, Danforth knows he's <u>lying</u>. Danforth doesn't want Proctor making a <u>mockery</u> of him — his main concern is still his <u>reputation</u>.

The judges make a <u>mistake</u> in bringing Rebecca in to <u>witness</u> Proctor's confession. Her bravery is <u>part</u> of what persuades Proctor <u>not to confess</u>.

Theme — Identity

For Proctor, his name isn't just about his <u>reputation</u> and <u>position</u> in the village, but also <u>who he is</u> and how he sees himself. He realises that if he signs his name to a lie, he'll lose his <u>self-respect</u>.

3) Proctor finally realises that he's a <u>good man</u>, and so he <u>can't</u> confess to something he hasn't done. He also thinks that confessing would mean <u>betraying</u> the other prisoners — he doesn't want to "blacken" their names while they "hang for their silence". His <u>conscience</u> can't cope with this which is why he withdraws his confession.

4) Hale thinks Proctor's decision stems from <u>pride</u>, but Elizabeth <u>refuses</u> to try to change Proctor's mind — she'd rather he died <u>happy</u> and able to see a "shred of goodness" in himself than have him confess and <u>live a lie</u>.

Stage directions

The morning sun <u>symbolises hope</u> — it suggests that the deaths will <u>end</u> the witch trials and eventually lead to a fundamental <u>change</u> in the <u>theocratic society</u> that allowed them to happen.

KEY QUOTE

"He have his goodness now. God forbid I take it from him!"

It might seem crazy that Elizabeth would rather see her husband die than live with the shame of a false confession. But as she sees it, he's saving himself from Hell. Still, it can't have been an easy decision.

Practice Questions

Well, that's the end of this section. I'm going to call it "My brief but very helpful guide to what happens in 'The Crucible' by Arthur Miller". At least until I think of something a bit catchier. Have a go at answering these questions to make sure you're completely clear about the play's plot.

Quick Questions — Act One

1) Whose daughter's 'illness' starts the village worrying about witchcraft?

2) Why did Elizabeth Proctor sack Abigail?

3) What have Putnam and Proctor fallen out over?

4) Why is Tituba one of the first people Abigail accuses of witchcraft?

5) Why does Abigail confess to having seen the Devil?

Quick Questions — Act Two

1) What's the relationship between John and Elizabeth Proctor like at the start of Act Two?

2) Find two examples in the stage directions of Mary's erratic behaviour.

3) Which of the Ten Commandments can't John remember? Why is this important?

4) What does the fact Hale goes to Proctor's house without the authority of the court say about him?

5) Why doesn't Hale try to stop the accusations at this point?

Practice Questions

Hopefully those questions about Acts One and Two weren't so bad. If you struggled with any of them, have a look back at the section to remind yourself about what happened. If you raced through them all as quickly as a speedy thing, then have a go at these questions about Acts Three and Four.

Quick Questions — Act Three

1) Why is it dangerous for John Proctor to challenge the court?

2) How many people sign the testimony?

3) Why does John admit that he had an affair with Abigail?

4) Why does Elizabeth deny that John had an affair with Abigail?

5) What form does Abigail claim Mary's spirit has taken?

Quick Questions — Act Four

1) What does Tituba mistake for the call of the Devil that suggests that she's been driven mad?

2) Why won't Danforth postpone John and Rebecca's hangings?

3) Hale and Parris both want to persuade the prisoners to confess.
   What are their different reasons for wanting the prisoners' lives saved?

4) Who robbed Parris and vanished?

5) Why won't Elizabeth persuade John to confess?

Section Three — Characters

Character Profile — John Proctor

John Proctor is the tragic hero of the play — a bit like Macbeth or Hamlet. He's not perfect, but he tries to do what he thinks is right — which makes it easy to relate to him...

John Proctor's a respected farmer...

1) Miller describes Proctor as having a "quiet confidence" which makes him "<u>respected</u> and even <u>feared</u>". You see this when he enters Betty's room in Act One — Mary and Mercy are <u>scared</u> of him.

2) The other characters <u>respect</u> him — Hale has an air of *"deference"* when he questions him in Act Two, and <u>Parris</u> admits that Proctor is one of the few people who have "<u>great weight</u>" in Salem.

> **Proctor is...**
>
> **brave:** "I will fall like an ocean on that court!"
>
> **blunt:** "I like not the smell of this 'authority'."
>
> **hot-tempered:** "Damn the Deputy Governor! Out of my house!"
>
> **tormented by guilt:** "I cannot mount the gibbet like a saint."

© 20thC.Fox/Everett/Rex Features

... but some people don't like him

1) Proctor's not afraid to <u>speak his mind</u>, which means that he has <u>enemies</u>:

> • He doesn't go to <u>church</u> very often and he makes it clear that he <u>doesn't like Parris</u> — he claims that Parris's sermons "hardly ever mention God".
>
> • He's not afraid to <u>challenge authority</u>. He stands up to <u>Putnam</u> — telling him that people vote "by name... not by acreage".

2) He also speaks his mind about the <u>court</u> — "you know in all your black hearts that this be fraud". He's overwhelmed by <u>anger</u> and <u>frustration</u> that he can't get the court to see <u>sense</u>.

> **Theme — Identity**
>
> Miller shows that although Proctor isn't afraid to <u>contradict</u> the authorities he isn't powerful enough to pose a <u>threat</u> to the community. This suggests that Miller didn't believe that those people McCarthy accused of <u>communism</u> were <u>dangerous</u> either.

Proctor's enemies are only too happy to discredit him when they get the chance.

Proctor is full of self-doubt

1) Proctor's basically a <u>good person</u>, but he has a <u>fatal flaw</u> — <u>lust</u>.

2) Although he's ended his <u>affair</u> with Abigail, and <u>confessed</u> to Elizabeth, he <u>can't forgive himself</u>.

> In some ways Proctor's lust <u>causes</u> the witch trials. If he hadn't had an affair with Abigail, she wouldn't have wanted <u>revenge</u> on his wife for chucking her out of the house — so he's partly <u>responsible</u> for what happens.

> **Theme — Identity**
>
> Proctor was drawn to Abigail, who's <u>passionate</u> and <u>immoral</u> — this shows that there's a side of him that <u>doesn't</u> want to follow the <u>rules</u> of society.

3) Proctor's angry at <u>himself</u> for being unfaithful, but at times he directs his anger at <u>Elizabeth</u>. This puts <u>strain</u> on their relationship.

Character Profile — John Proctor

Proctor undergoes a fairly major journey — at the start of the play he's full of doubt and self-loathing, but by the end he's realised that he's a good man. It's not an easy ride, though...

He's a complex character

There are lots of <u>different sides</u> to Proctor:

Proctor isn't all good or all bad — this makes him more believable as a character.

1) He's got a <u>short temper</u>, which means he sometimes acts <u>impulsively</u> — for example, he <u>tears</u> up the <u>warrant</u> for Elizabeth's arrest. At other times he <u>thinks carefully</u> before he acts — for example when he <u>puts off</u> telling the court that Abigail's lying.

© AJ Chan

2) He can be <u>violent</u> — he <u>threatens</u> to <u>beat</u> Mary Warren for leaving the house. At other times he's <u>kind</u> — such as when he <u>protects</u> Mary from Parris's questions in court.

3) He <u>respects God</u>, but sees that the Church <u>isn't always right</u>. He lives by <u>his own moral code</u>, rather than by the rules in the Bible.

Theme — Identity

Proctor's character represents the <u>struggle</u> faced by people in Salem — they wanted to be <u>individuals</u>, but it was much <u>safer</u> to <u>obey</u> the church's <u>rules</u>.

Proctor faces a lot of tough choices

1) Proctor's <u>reluctant</u> to tell the town that Abigail's <u>lying</u> — he knows that if he does she might <u>expose</u> their <u>affair</u>. But once the court starts hanging people, he realises he <u>doesn't have a choice</u>.

2) <u>Elizabeth's arrest</u> forces Proctor to take action — he isn't prepared to <u>let her die</u> for his sins. He tells Mary Warren, "My wife will never die for me!" — this shows that he'll <u>risk his own life</u> to save Elizabeth's.

3) Proctor has the chance to keep <u>out of trouble</u> when Danforth tells him that Elizabeth's pregnant, and <u>won't be hanged</u> for at least a year. He decides to tell the court that Abigail's lying — he <u>can't</u> leave the <u>other</u> prisoners to be <u>hanged</u>.

4) Proctor's hardest choice is whether he should <u>confess</u> to <u>save his life</u>:

- At first he confesses — he doesn't think he's <u>good</u> enough to die "like a saint".

- He finally sees that confessing will destroy his <u>self-respect</u> — and realising that he still respects himself makes him recognise his own <u>goodness</u>. He <u>tears up</u> his confession.

Historical Background

Proctor could represent Miller or others who were accused of communism. They had to <u>decide</u> whether to <u>accuse</u> their friends or remain <u>loyal</u> to them.

Theme — Loyalty

Proctor is <u>loyal</u> to his <u>friends</u> and his own <u>moral code</u> — he won't do something he thinks is <u>wrong</u>, just because he's <u>told</u> that it's <u>right</u>.

Proctor asks whether Rebecca Nurse or Martha Corey have confessed — if they had it would mean that his confession wouldn't betray them. They haven't, which strengthens his resolve not to confess.

KEY QUOTE

"The magistrate sits in your heart that judges you."

As Elizabeth points out, Proctor's really hard on himself. Part of the tragedy of the play is that when he finally sees the "shred of goodness in John Proctor" he sticks to his morals, and that leads to his death.

Character Profile — Elizabeth Proctor

Miller doesn't write a potted history of Elizabeth like he does for the other characters, but her actions say a lot about her. She stays strong and loyal through everything, even when the rest of Salem seems to have gone mad.

Elizabeth represents loyalty and conscience

Elizabeth is...

loyal: "My husband – is a goodly man".

honest: "In her life, sir, she have never lied."

clear-sighted: "She has an arrow in you yet, John Proctor".

© AJ Chan

1) Elizabeth's <u>first priority</u> is her <u>children</u> — when she's arrested, her first reaction is to ask Proctor to tell them that she's "gone to visit someone sick", so they <u>won't be frightened</u>.

2) Despite Proctor's affair, she's <u>fiercely loyal</u> to him — when asked about his <u>affair</u> in court, she <u>denies</u> it to <u>save his reputation</u>, even though she believes she's <u>damning herself</u> by lying.

3) She encourages Proctor to tell the court that Abigail's <u>lying</u> — even though by attacking Abigail she runs the risk that Abigail will <u>reveal</u> her <u>affair</u> with Proctor.

 Theme — Conscience
Elizabeth is more concerned about <u>stopping</u> the girls <u>accusing people</u> than about her <u>own happiness</u>.

She's very religious and very moral

1) Elizabeth takes <u>pride</u> in being a "covenanted Christian woman". When Hale asks her if she knows the Ten Commandments, she replies "*eagerly*" — she's keen to show that she's a <u>good Christian</u>.

2) However, Elizabeth <u>hasn't</u> insisted on her third son being <u>baptised</u>, because she <u>dislikes</u> Parris. Like Proctor, Elizabeth acts as she <u>believes is right</u>, rather than as <u>society</u> tells her she should act.

3) Proctor says several times that Elizabeth <u>never lies</u>. In Act Two, she tells Hale that she <u>doesn't believe</u> in witches — this is a good example of her <u>telling the truth</u>, despite the <u>danger</u> it could put her in.

Elizabeth's weakness is her insecurity

1) In Act Two it's clear that Elizabeth <u>distrusts</u> Proctor, which is <u>destroying</u> their marriage.

2) In Act Four, Elizabeth admits that she <u>didn't believe</u> that Proctor could really <u>love</u> her because she was "<u>plain</u>". Her <u>doubts</u> caused her to act <u>coldly</u> towards him.

Theme — Loyalty
Elizabeth admits her own <u>faults</u> to Proctor to make him see that even good people make mistakes. She takes some of the <u>blame</u> for the fact he cheated to try and make him feel <u>less guilty</u> and to show John that <u>having flaws</u> doesn't stop him from being a <u>good man</u>.

Character Profile — Elizabeth Proctor

Miller's saying something about human nature by showing some characters — like Elizabeth — learning from their mistakes, while others — like the judges — are as narrow-minded at the end as they are at the start.

Elizabeth reflects other people's guilty consciences

Elizabeth gets criticised a lot by the other characters, but the things they say about her often seem to be quite accurate descriptions of themselves. For example:

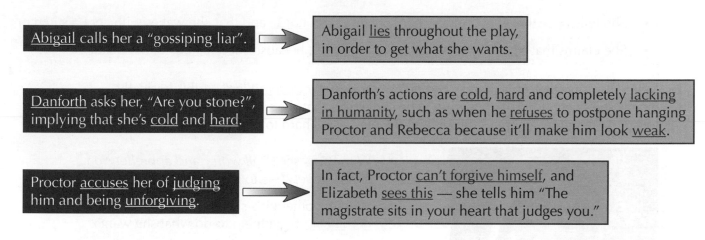

Abigail calls her a "gossiping liar".	→	Abigail lies throughout the play, in order to get what she wants.
Danforth asks her, "Are you stone?", implying that she's cold and hard.	→	Danforth's actions are cold, hard and completely lacking in humanity, such as when he refuses to postpone hanging Proctor and Rebecca because it'll make him look weak.
Proctor accuses her of judging him and being unforgiving.	→	In fact, Proctor can't forgive himself, and Elizabeth sees this — she tells him "The magistrate sits in your heart that judges you."

She changes during the play

1) In Act Two, Elizabeth's treatment of Proctor makes her seem cold. She claims that she's forgiven him, but it's clear that she doesn't trust him, e.g. she says "you are not open with me". She also keeps him at a distance, such as when she "*receives*" his kiss, rather than welcoming it.

2) By Act Four, Elizabeth has taken the blame for Proctor's affair, admitting that she kept a "cold house". She recognises her own failings.

3) She forgives Proctor and tells him she'll support him whether he confesses or not. She sees that he has to come to his own decision, and doesn't try to persuade him either way.

4) At the end of the play, there is real love and passion between Proctor and Elizabeth — admitting their own shortcomings has helped them overcome their problems.

Language

Have a look at how cold and stilted Elizabeth's speech is in Act Two, and how warm and natural it is in Act Four. This shows how much she's changed.

© Felicity Peacock

Theme — Conscience and Loyalty

Elizabeth wants Proctor to live, but she believes that confessing to Devil worship would damn him. She won't ask him to confess because she values his soul above her own happiness.

EXAM TIP

Explain why Elizabeth and John are well-suited...

You should mention that the Proctors have some pretty serious problems, but you'll impress the examiner if you also say how they're well-suited. They both fight for what they believe in, even if it means they'll suffer.

Character Profile — Abigail Williams

Abigail's not the most complicated of characters — basically she's completely unscrupulous and will stop at nothing to get her own way. Y'know, I kind of admire the girl...

Abigail's beautiful but dishonest

1) Miller describes Abigail as "<u>strikingly beautiful</u>" — something that she <u>uses</u> to her advantage. Abigail refers to her <u>beauty</u> and <u>sexuality</u> several times, showing how <u>vain</u> and <u>self-obsessed</u> she is, for example:

- She tells Hale that Tituba makes her "dream <u>corruptions</u>" and that she wakes with "<u>not a stitch on</u>".

- She claims that Mary's spirit wants to <u>tear her face</u>, because she's <u>jealous</u> of her beauty.

2) Miller also says that Abigail has "*an endless capacity for <u>dissembling</u>*" — this basically means she's very good at <u>appearing</u> to be something that she's <u>not</u>. She seems to have lots of <u>different personalities</u> throughout the play — it's hard to tell which of them is <u>real</u>:

- With Parris she's "*all worry and apprehension and propriety*" — to show she's <u>innocent</u>.

- With the other girls she's <u>bullying</u> and <u>dominant</u>, to get them to do what she wants.

- With Proctor she's <u>flirty</u> and <u>passionate</u>, to try to win him back. When that doesn't work she <u>cries</u> to make him <u>pity</u> her.

Abigail is...

heartless: "She thinks to dance with me on my wife's grave!"

a liar: "She sends her spirit on me in church"

a bully: "I'll beat you, Betty!"

© 20TH CENTURY FOX / THE KOBAL COLLECTION / WETCHER, BARRY

She'll do anything to get out of trouble

Abigail can't risk her reputation being damaged — if it is, she'll find it difficult to get married, so she'll never have any independence.

1) Abigail's position in society is <u>uncertain</u> — she's an orphan, so she's <u>dependent</u> on Parris until she marries. She can't risk him finding out that she'd had an <u>affair</u> with Proctor or thinking that she's practised <u>witchcraft</u>.

2) In Act One Parris has caught her <u>dancing</u> in the forest, and has heard rumours that her reputation is "<u>soiled</u>". Hale also seems to think that she's <u>hiding something</u>, but Abigail quickly sees a way out — she <u>accuses Tituba</u> of witchcraft and <u>shifts attention</u> from herself.

3) When accusing Tituba works, Abigail cements her new role as a <u>victim of witchcraft</u> by <u>accusing</u> other villagers of bewitching her.

Theme — Intolerance

All the people Abigail accuses <u>early on</u> are on the <u>edge</u> of society — she knows she wouldn't be believed if she named <u>respectable</u> people at this stage, so instead she names people who are <u>slaves</u>, <u>homeless</u>, <u>drunks</u> etc. She knows that nobody will bother <u>defending</u> them.

4) In Act Four, we find out that Abigail has <u>stolen money</u> and <u>run away</u> — she's realised that her popularity <u>won't last long</u> once people like Proctor and Rebecca are hanged, so she gets out while she can.

Character Profile — Abigail Williams

It's easy to write Abigail off as a vicious, calculating murderer, but you need to know a bit about her background to understand why she's the way she is...

Abigail's good at manipulating people

Theme — Identity

Abigail sees herself as a bit of a rebel — she says to Proctor "a wild thing may say wild things", suggesting that she thinks she's different from the other people in the village, and justified in breaking their rules.

1) Abigail soon realises that accusing people gives her power and makes people pay attention to her.

2) Abigail mixes her lies with bits of truth to make them more believable. For example, she claims that Tituba makes her "laugh at prayer". Since she's been in trouble for laughing during prayer, this is taken as proof of Tituba's guilt.

3) She's clever and ruthless. In Act One, she hears Hale saying that a "sudden cold wind" or a "bird invisible to others" are signs of witchcraft. She uses these two things to convince the judges that Mary's a witch in Act Three.

Theme — Revenge

For Abigail, accusing people of witchcraft is a chance to get revenge on people she thinks have spread rumours about her. More importantly, she wants to get rid of Elizabeth so she can marry Proctor herself.

There are some excuses for Abigail's nastiness

It might seem like Abigail's pure evil, but you need to bear in mind that she hasn't had the easiest life:

- She's an orphan — she claims she "saw Indians smash my dear parents' heads on the pillow next to mine".

- Parris is described as having "no interest in children, or talent with them" — he wouldn't have provided a warm or loving home for Abigail.

- As a young, unmarried girl she has no power, so nobody pays any attention to her — which must be difficult for someone as vain and attention-seeking as she is.

- Life in Salem is repressive — for a young, passionate girl, only being allowed to work and pray must be pretty dull.

- She falls in love with Proctor, but he rejects her. Their affair showed her what it was like to have someone care about her, and she can't be satisfied with her old life now.

© AJ Chan

KEY QUOTE

"What look do you give me? ... I'll not have such looks!"

Abigail may be a ruthless bully, but you've got to admit, she's also pretty gutsy. She stabs herself with that pin to frame Elizabeth, and when she's accused of lying in Act Three she even dares to threaten Danforth.

Character Profile — Reverend John Hale

Poor old Hale — he means well, but things go horribly wrong for him.

Hale is a witchcraft expert — which makes him a bit cocky

1) Miller describes Hale as an "eager-eyed intellectual". He's proud of his knowledge and wants to show it off.

2) He believes in witchcraft, but unlike the other characters he approaches things with an open mind — he refuses to examine Betty unless people promise to believe him if he finds that her illness isn't caused by witchcraft.

3) When the girls start accusing people, he takes it as proof of his own ability — he doesn't consider that they might be lying.

Hale is...

fair: "What I have heard in her favour, I will not fear to testify"

proud: "he felt the pride of the specialist"

compassionate: "I would save your husband's life"

guilt-stricken: "There is blood on my head!"

© AJ Chan

Theme — Religion

At first, Hale is blinded by his faith — he's so convinced the girls are bewitched that he doesn't think about what they might gain from accusing people. Later, he tells Proctor that "the light of God" must be in Parris, because he's a minister — he believes Parris is doing God's work, rather than acting for his own benefit.

He tries to make up for his mistakes — but it's too late

Theme — Loyalty

Unlike the other authority figures, Hale is loyal to his own idea of right and wrong. Rather than trying to protect his reputation, he admits his mistakes and tries to stop the prisoners from being hanged.

1) Hale's fair-minded in court, and tries to persuade the judges to listen to Proctor and Giles's evidence.

2) He stands up to Danforth when he believes he's wrong — he asks him to "stop now before another is condemned".

3) When he knows for certain that the girls are lying, he storms out of the court in protest at Proctor's arrest.

He abandons his principles

1) Hale tries to persuade the prisoners to confess to save their lives — he knows the confessions are false, and believes that he'll be damned for telling them to lie.

2) Hale argues that "life is God's most precious gift", and that it's a sin for the prisoners to throw their lives away by refusing to confess.

3) But he has less courage than a character like John Proctor, who's prepared to die for what he believes in.

Theme — Conscience

You could argue that Hale tries to save the prisoners' lives to ease his guilt at the part he played in the trials.

KEY QUOTE

"He is steeped in sorrow"

Hale probably changes more than any other character — he feels guilty, frustrated and "exhausted" by the end of the trial. He learns that people and morality are more complicated than Puritan teachings suggest.

Character Profile — Parris & the Putnams

Ugghh, just thinking about these three makes my whole body shudder with fear and loathing...

Reverend Parris is in the wrong job

1) Parris is a <u>minister</u>, but he's <u>not</u> a <u>spiritual</u> man. When he suspects his daughter and niece have been practising witchcraft, his main concern is for his <u>reputation</u> and <u>job</u> — not for their <u>souls</u>.

2) He's <u>materialistic</u> — Proctor says that "for twenty week he preach nothin' but golden candlesticks".

3) Parris is a <u>representative of God</u>, which gives him a lot of <u>power</u>. Despite this, it's clear that nobody really <u>respects</u> him — Proctor and Giles openly <u>challenge</u> him and the judges <u>don't listen</u> to him. This is a sign that, even before the witch trials, the power of <u>theocracy</u> is <u>declining</u>.

4) He's also <u>self-serving</u> — for example, in court he <u>bad mouths</u> Proctor, who he feels <u>threatened</u> by.

5) Parris is <u>cowardly</u> and <u>selfish</u> to the end. He pleads for Proctor and Rebecca's hangings to be <u>postponed</u> because he's scared there'll be a <u>riot</u>, and that he might be a <u>target</u>.

> **Theme — Fear**
>
> Parris uses <u>fear</u> to stop people <u>questioning</u> his <u>authority</u> — he tells Proctor, "There is either obedience or the church will burn like Hell".

By making Parris so shallow and petty, Miller highlights the problems with a theocratic society.

The Putnams are bitter and vindictive

© AJ Chan

1) The Putnams are one of the most <u>powerful</u> families in Salem. They think this makes them <u>better</u> than other people.

> **Theme — Envy and Revenge**
>
> The Putnams have lots of <u>grievances</u> against people in Salem and want to see them <u>punished</u>. For example, they <u>argued</u> with the Nurses over <u>land boundaries</u> and who should be <u>minister</u> — it's no coincidence that it's the Putnams who accuse <u>Rebecca Nurse</u> of witchcraft.

2) They're <u>respectable</u> members of the community and seem to support Parris, but they use their power to try to <u>control</u> him. For example, they encourage him to call in Hale — they know that consulting a witchcraft expert will <u>provoke hysteria</u> in Salem.

3) The Putnams <u>want</u> other villagers to be <u>accused</u> of witchcraft because it <u>supports</u> their belief that their children were <u>killed by witchcraft</u>, and gives them the chance to <u>buy the land</u> of those accused:

- Putnam uses <u>fear</u> to start the accusations — he says Tituba "must be <u>hanged</u>" if she won't confess.

- He makes his <u>daughter</u> accuse people whose land he wants — if they plead guilty they <u>lose their land</u>, if they plead not guilty they're <u>hanged</u> — <u>either way</u> their land is up for grabs.

EXAM TIP

Think about why Miller makes some characters so nasty...

It's no accident that Parris and the Putnams are so awful. Miller makes those in power more unlikeable to highlight the hypocrisy of Salem and the courage and goodness of people like Proctor and Rebecca.

Character Profile — The Victims

All in all, nineteen people were hanged during the Salem witch trials. Miller focuses on a few of them to give the audience a better idea of what their characters are like, and to make us sympathise with them more.

Giles Corey is brave and loyal

1) Miller describes Giles Corey as "the most <u>comical hero</u> in the history" — he provides a few moments of <u>light relief</u>.

2) He doesn't know when to <u>keep quiet</u>, and is involved in lots of <u>disputes</u> over land boundaries. However, he emerges as one of the <u>strongest</u> and <u>most likeable</u> characters in the play.

3) Giles <u>refuses</u> to plead guilty or not guilty, so that his sons can <u>inherit</u> his land. This is <u>more important</u> to him than his <u>reputation</u> — he's a <u>practical</u> man.

> **Theme — Loyalty**
>
> Giles <u>refuses</u> to say who told him that Thomas Putnam was accusing people so that he could buy their land. He's prepared to face <u>arrest</u> rather than <u>betray a friend</u>.

Miller presents Rebecca Nurse as almost saintly

1) Rebecca's very <u>wise</u> — she advises the other characters that the girls are going through "silly seasons", and that there's "prodigious danger in the seeking of loose spirits". Miller uses her <u>wisdom</u> and <u>foresight</u> to <u>foreshadow</u> later events, which builds <u>tension</u>.

2) She's a <u>peacemaker</u> — e.g. she tells Proctor that he can't "break charity" with Parris.

3) It's partly the <u>sight</u> of Rebecca going <u>bravely</u> to her death at the end of Act Four that makes Proctor <u>withdraw his confession</u>.

> **Themes — Religion and Identity**
>
> <u>Religion</u> is a crucial part of who Rebecca is — she firmly believes that if she <u>breaks</u> the Ten Commandments, she'll be <u>damned</u>. She'd rather be <u>hanged</u> for a crime she didn't commit than risk her <u>soul</u>, so she doesn't consider confessing.

Tituba is the first person to be accused

1) As a <u>slave</u>, Tituba has a <u>low status</u>. When Abigail accuses her of witchcraft, she sees that she'll be <u>killed</u> unless she confesses.

2) She uses her confession to vent her <u>dislike</u> of <u>Parris</u> — she tells them the Devil said, "Mr Parris no goodly man, Mr Parris mean man". By quoting the Devil, she's able to express her <u>own feelings</u> about Parris in a way she wouldn't normally be able to. Her words give an insight into how she's been treated, and may help explain her <u>readiness</u> to <u>accuse white people</u>.

© Moviestore Collection Ltd

> **Themes — Intolerance and Fear**
>
> Tituba does have some knowledge of <u>magic</u>, but she only uses it to make <u>harmless</u> charms for the girls. The other villagers <u>fear the unknown</u> too much to let her explain this, so they believe Abigail when she accuses Tituba.

EXAM TIP

Pay attention to what the minor characters get up to...

You probably won't get a question focusing on these characters, but you still need to know what they do in the play, why they act the way they do and what Miller is trying to show through their actions and motives.

Character Profile — The Girls

And so to the girls. They're a lovely bunch of sweet, innocent little things. Oh no, I meant the opposite — they're a malicious and cold-hearted bunch of murderous fiends. Still, I'll let you form your own opinion.

The girls fear getting into trouble

1) Although the girls are on the <u>margins</u> of Salem society, they form their own <u>mini community</u>. The <u>main role</u> they play is to <u>accuse</u> people of bewitching them. Because they're acting as a <u>group</u>, they're very <u>convincing</u> — they <u>fool</u> the judges and drive the whole town to <u>hysteria</u>.

2) Abigail's the group's <u>ringleader</u>. For example, in Act Three she's the first to mention a "cold wind", and the other girls <u>copy</u> her — "I freeze!"

3) Puritan society was very <u>strict</u>, and children were expected to <u>obey adults</u> without question. This makes the girls more likely to obey a <u>strong leader</u> like Abigail.

© AJ Chan

Theme — Fear

The girls <u>broke the rules</u> by practising witchcraft, and they're <u>scared</u> of getting into trouble for it. This reflects the way that people in Salem are tired of obeying the <u>strict rules</u> of the <u>church</u>, but are <u>frightened</u> to be seen to have broken them.

Miller doesn't give the girls strong individual identities

Theme — Identity

Despite the <u>power</u> the court gives the girls, in Act Three they <u>lose their identities</u> even more — the judges call them "the girls" or "the children" and they <u>speak as one</u>.

1) Miller describes each girl in just a <u>few words</u> — Susanna Walcott is "a <u>nervous</u>, <u>hurried</u> girl", and Betty Parris is simply "aged <u>ten</u>". Their <u>personalities</u> and <u>youth</u> explain how Abigail <u>intimidates</u> them so easily.

2) Miller describes Mercy Lewis as a "fat, sly, <u>merciless</u> girl" — her personality is the <u>opposite</u> of her name. She helps Abigail <u>bully</u> Mary and Betty in Act One, and is the first to <u>back her up</u> in court.

Mary Warren tries to do the right thing

1) Mary Warren is a "subservient, naïve, lonely girl". She <u>tries</u> to stand up for herself, but she's too <u>weak</u>.

2) She's <u>easily influenced</u> by others — she explains that, when the other girls screamed and everyone believed them, she too <u>believed</u> that she could see spirits. This is called the <u>power of suggestion</u> — it probably explains some of the <u>other girls'</u> actions too.

3) She tries to tell the court that Abigail's <u>lying</u>, but Abigail's far <u>stronger</u> than Mary. She uses <u>fear</u> and <u>peer pressure</u> to get Mary to give in.

Peer pressure is the urge to change your behaviour to conform to a social group.

Theme — Fear

By Act Three, the girls are so <u>powerful</u> that they can accuse <u>anyone</u> of <u>anything</u> and be believed. No wonder Mary's <u>frightened</u> out of her wits.

"Oh, Mary, this is a black art to change your shape."

In court, Abigail and the girls play on Mary's fears of being hanged and of being an outsider until she eventually has a complete breakdown and can't tell fact from fiction. They're a dreadful gang of bullies.

Character Profile — Deputy-Governor Danforth

Apparently Arthur Miller saw the two judges — Danforth and Hathorne — as the real villains of *The Crucible*, and wished he'd made them come across as even more evil. They already seem pretty evil to me...

Danforth is very powerful

© 20thC.Fox/Everett/Rex Features

Danforth is...

arrogant: "Do you know who I am, Mr Nurse?"

prejudiced: "the voice of Heaven is speaking through the children"

uncaring: "I should hang ten thousand that dared to rise against the law"

1) Danforth is the <u>Deputy Governor</u> of Massachusetts — he's <u>very important</u>. He's the <u>main judge</u> in *The Crucible*.

2) He has "*an <u>exact loyalty</u> to his position and his cause*" — he <u>believes totally</u> in what he's doing, and <u>wants</u> to find people guilty because it supports his beliefs. This makes him <u>narrow-minded</u>.

3) Miller describes Danforth as a man of "humour and sophistication". Unfortunately these good qualities are <u>buried</u> by <u>loyalty</u> to his <u>job</u>.

4) Danforth's <u>intelligence</u> and <u>experience</u> makes the fact that he's <u>taken in</u> by the girls' accusations even more <u>frightening</u>.

Theme — Identity

Danforth is convinced of his own <u>importance</u>. He's so certain he's right that he doesn't like being <u>questioned</u>.

He's worried about people attacking the court

Theme — Intolerance

Danforth's believes that what he's doing is <u>right</u>, and anybody who <u>challenges</u> him must have something to <u>hide</u>.

1) At first, Danforth seems like a <u>reasonable</u> man — he <u>listens</u> to the <u>evidence</u> brought by Proctor, Giles and Francis, and seems to consider it. He sees himself as <u>fair-minded</u>, but he's actually <u>biased</u> in favour of the girls.

2) He <u>identifies</u> so strongly with the <u>court</u> that he sees any attack on it as an attack on <u>himself</u>. When Proctor refuses to drop the charge against Abigail, Danforth claims that Proctor's "purpose is <u>somewhat larger</u>" — he assumes that he's trying to <u>overthrow</u> the court and <u>destroy his reputation</u>.

Theme — Fear

In Act Three, you could argue that Danforth's <u>misguided</u>. However, in Act Four when it becomes obvious that the accusations are <u>false</u>, he still <u>refuses</u> to stop the hangings because he's afraid it will make him appear <u>weak</u>.

He doesn't understand human nature

1) Danforth can't accept that the girls are <u>lying</u>. He's too <u>arrogant</u> to admit that they've <u>fooled him</u>.

2) He takes the confessions at <u>face value</u>, instead of seeing that people are only confessing to <u>save their lives</u> — when Hale protests that the prisoners are innocent, Danforth replies "I'll hear no more of that!"

KEY QUOTE *"No uncorrupted man may fear this court"*

Danforth sees all who disagree with the court as a threat — like McCarthy saw anyone with different political views as a threat. Danforth is a horrible character — showing that Miller disliked such narrow-mindedness.

Character Profile — Hathorne, Cheever & Herrick

Hathorne is the other judge who appears alongside Danforth — he's not as important, but he's just as nasty. Cheever and Herrick are court officials — they pretty much just do as they're told.

Hathorne has no redeeming features

1) Like Danforth, Hathorne is <u>fanatical</u> about people <u>respecting</u> the <u>court's power</u>, and <u>paranoid</u> that people are trying to <u>overthrow</u> it.

2) But unlike Danforth, Hathorne <u>isn't</u> completely <u>secure</u> in his own power — this makes him even more <u>merciless</u>.

3) To prevent the court being <u>undermined</u>, he tries to <u>suppress the evidence</u> that Proctor, Giles and Francis bring. He can't arrest people without Danforth's permission, so he continually <u>asks</u> Danforth to <u>arrest anyone</u> who speaks <u>out of turn</u>.

4) The only time that Hathorne shows any <u>emotion</u> is when Proctor confesses — he's <u>joyful</u> because Proctor's confession will make people believe that the <u>others</u> are <u>guilty</u> too.

© Geraint Lewis / Alamy

Ezekiel Cheever is the court clerk

1) Cheever's main appearance in the play is when he <u>arrests Elizabeth</u>. He takes his <u>duty</u> very seriously — he says "I must do as I'm told", and doesn't seem to consider that anyone charged with witchcraft could be <u>innocent</u>.

2) The fact that he comes to arrest Elizabeth is <u>shocking</u>, because she has just asked Proctor to tell Cheever that the girls' illness has "naught to do with witchcraft" — she <u>trusts</u> Cheever to <u>see sense</u> and stop the witchcraft trials.

3) Cheever speaks "*apologetically*" and "*kindly*" to Proctor when he tells the court that Proctor ploughs on Sundays, and that he ripped up the <u>warrant</u> for Elizabeth's arrest. But despite his regret and kindness, his <u>sense of duty</u> means that he feels he has to tell the judges <u>everything</u> he knows. His <u>respect</u> for the court is so <u>unconditional</u> that he <u>can't see</u> the bigger picture — that he's helping to hang innocent people.

Theme — Identity

Like the <u>judges</u>, Cheever <u>identifies</u> himself solely in terms of his <u>job</u>. If anyone <u>questions</u> the court, he sees it as his <u>duty</u> to make sure they're <u>punished</u>.

Herrick is Salem's marshal

1) Herrick is also responsible for <u>arresting Elizabeth</u> — but he is "somewhat <u>shamefaced</u>" when he does, suggesting that he is <u>less comfortable</u> arresting his friends and neighbours than Cheever is.

2) He tries to <u>stick up</u> for Proctor in court, telling Danforth that he's "a good man". He also treats Tituba and Sarah Good <u>kindly</u> in jail.

3) All the same, he <u>does as he's told</u> and <u>doesn't try</u> to change things, even when he sees they're <u>wrong</u>.

Explain how the court officials represent blind loyalty...

Miller uses the court officials to show the dangers of misplaced loyalty — the officials are so loyal to the court that, even when it's destroying their community and killing their neighbours, they never question its decisions.

Practice Questions

You should now know everything there is to know about the characters in 'The Crucible'. Make sure you're on track by having a go at these quick questions, then when you're ready, try your hand at the slightly trickier questions on the next page.

Quick Questions

1) Give one reason why some people in Salem don't like John Proctor.

2) What is John Proctor's fatal flaw?

3) When Elizabeth is arrested, why does she ask Proctor to tell the children she's visiting a sick person?

4) Why does Proctor think that Elizabeth won't lie in court?

5) Give one reason why Abigail accuses Elizabeth Proctor of witchcraft.

6) Whose arrest causes Hale to storm out of the court?

7) Give one example of how Parris is selfish.

8) Name two things that the Putnams argued with Rebecca and Francis Nurse about.

9) Why does Giles Corey refuse to plead guilty or not guilty?

10) Give one quote from the play that supports the idea that Rebecca Nurse is wise.

11) Why is Abigail able to control the other girls so easily?

12) What does Danforth believe Proctor is trying to do by accusing Abigail of lying?

Practice Questions

I'm not going to lie to you — these questions aren't going to be easy. But they're the best practice you can have for your exam, so it's worth spending some time on them. Don't try to answer all the exam-style questions in one go — it'll make your head explode. Do them one at a time, but try to do them under exam conditions if you can — it may seem like a chore but it's the best practice you can do.

In-depth Questions

1) How do you think Proctor's feelings for Abigail differ at the start and end of the play?

2) Explain how Elizabeth represents the theme of loyalty in *The Crucible*.

3) Do you think Hale takes responsibility for his mistakes? Explain your answer.

4) Make a list of Mary Warren's actions throughout the play.
For each action, briefly explain what motivates her to act in that way.

5) Do you think Danforth is a coward? Explain your answer.

6) Why do the Putnams pretend to support Parris? What are their real feelings towards him?

Exam-style Questions

1) To what extent is John Proctor a good man?

2) Abigail Williams describes Elizabeth Proctor as "cold". In your opinion, is Elizabeth a cold character? Justify your answer with examples from the text.

3) To what extent can Abigail be said to be responsible for the events of the play?

4) How does Arthur Miller present the character of Hale?

Religion and Intolerance

The characters in *The Crucible* are Puritans — they take the rules in the Bible at face value, and think religion should be simple and strict. They want everyone to agree with them — anyone who doesn't is seen as ungodly.

The Church is very powerful

1) Seventeenth-century Salem is a theocracy (see p.6). That basically means that laws are based on religious laws and the Church tells people how to behave.

2) The court sees itself as being guided by God — this gives it power to decide whether people are guilty, and how they should be punished.

3) This would be okay if the judges — Danforth and Hathorne — were honest and fair-minded, but they're not. They're motivated by the desire to protect their reputations.

4) They won't tolerate any challenges to their power, e.g. anyone questioning the court is immediately suspected of witchcraft.

© AJ Chan

People in Salem are intolerant of anyone who acts differently

1) Anyone in *The Crucible* who doesn't behave as the church tells them to is suspected of being influenced by the Devil. This makes them a threat to the church and the public.

2) This means that people try to hide their sins, so there are lots of secrets in Salem.

3) For example, when the girls are caught dancing (which is forbidden), they're too scared to admit it. Instead they lie to get out of trouble.

4) Hale is suspicious of the Proctors because he's heard a rumour that they "hold no belief" in witches — even thinking differently from other people is dangerous.

Lots of the evidence against the witches is based on rumour and hearsay — see page 38.

People eventually see how dangerous intolerance is

1) Miller wanted his audience to see how dangerous intolerance, fear of difference and being unwilling to change your viewpoint can be.

2) Some characters see how intolerant society in Salem is, and dislike it. Proctor represents the struggle between obedience to society and individual freedom. He thinks his own sense of right and wrong is more important than society's view.

3) By Act Four, many more characters see the problems with a repressive society and religious intolerance. This is partly because witch trials are also taking place in the nearby village of Andover, and there are rumours that the villagers there have succeeded in overturning the court.

4) By the end of the play, the characters who are driven by selfish motives (like the judges and Parris) are still blind to the dangers of intolerance. On the other hand, Hale recognises the problems that intolerance has caused and is trying to fight it — he provides hope that the church will eventually be more tolerant.

As people rebel against intolerance, the power of theocracy is threatened.

Mention how Miller links religion and intolerance...

You can impress the examiner by making connections between different themes in the play. You could write about how Miller portrays the rigid rules of Puritanism as a cause of the intolerance that led to the witch trials.

Envy and Revenge

Loads of the bad stuff that happens in the play is caused by people being jealous of each other, or trying to get their own back on people they think have wronged them in some way. They're a friendly bunch in Salem...

The witch trials bring out lots of buried grudges

1) Miller says that people in Salem have a "predilection for minding other people's business" — everyone knows what everyone else <u>gets up to</u> and people are expected to <u>report</u> any wrongdoing. This causes lots of <u>resentment</u> — so people use the <u>accusations</u> as a way of getting <u>revenge</u> on their neighbours.

2) <u>Tituba</u> is the first person accused — she says that the Devil tells her "I have *white* people belong to me". Her <u>emphasis</u> of the word *"white"* could suggest she's seeking revenge on people who have <u>mistreated</u> her.

> John Proctor says "vengeance is walking Salem". By <u>personifying</u> vengeance he makes it sound <u>frightening</u> and <u>powerful</u>.

3) Parris thinks he's "<u>persecuted</u>" by people like John Proctor and Giles Corey, so he tries to <u>discredit</u> them — he describes Giles as "contentious" (argumentative) and says that John is "mischief".

Abigail's motives are envy and revenge

1) Abigail's <u>jealous</u> of Elizabeth Proctor — she can't accept that Proctor loves Elizabeth, who she sees as <u>cold</u> and <u>weak</u>.

2) She's also <u>angry</u> that Elizabeth <u>sacked</u> her when she found out about the affair, and she wants <u>revenge</u> on her. It comes as no surprise when Abigail <u>accuses</u> Elizabeth of witchcraft — Elizabeth says she "<u>knew all week</u> it would come to this!"

3) Abigail knows the rest of the village <u>look down</u> on her. She knows people have been <u>gossiping</u> about her, so she grabs the opportunity to <u>punish</u> them by accusing them of witchcraft.

Abigail doesn't try to get revenge on John directly, even when he calls her a whore — she still hopes that with Elizabeth out of the way he'll marry her.

The Putnams see an opportunity to settle scores

1) The <u>Putnams</u> feel that the other residents of Salem <u>don't respect</u> them.

2) In Act One they seem <u>delighted</u> that the girls are ill — Goody Putnam is *"shiny-eyed"* as she describes Betty's illness as "a marvel". She sees that fears about <u>witchcraft</u> will <u>cause trouble</u> for Salem's residents.

3) They <u>make</u> their daughter Ruth <u>accuse</u> people in order to <u>settle scores</u>. For example, Ruth accuses <u>Rebecca Nurse</u> — the Putnams want revenge on the Nurses because of arguments over land (see page 29).

"common vengeance writes the law!"

As Proctor points out, Abigail and the others have hijacked the law with their thirst for revenge. Many characters use the witch hunts as a handy opportunity to get people they don't like into trouble.

Fear

People in Salem live in constant fear — of the Devil, of damnation, of what lurks in the wilderness and so on. Once the accusations start, these fears develop into hysteria, until everyone is terrified of everyone else.

There is a genuine fear of witchcraft

1) Many people in Salem believe that <u>witches</u> exist, and some think that they work for the <u>Devil</u> and want to <u>hurt</u> other people.

2) They live hard lives, and many <u>unexplained</u> things that happen — like floods, their crops failing, children dying — are seen as <u>punishment from God</u> or the <u>work of the Devil</u>.

3) People believe that if they <u>get rid of witches</u> the Devil will have <u>less power</u>, so their lives will be <u>better</u>.

4) But the genuinely 'good' people — like Rebecca, Giles and Elizabeth — <u>aren't scared</u> of witchcraft. Miller could be suggesting that people's <u>fear</u> of witchcraft is actually driven by their <u>guilty consciences</u>.

People are scared of being judged by their neighbours

1) People in Salem worry that if they're thought to have <u>sinned</u>, they'll be <u>judged</u> — not just by <u>God</u>, but by their <u>neighbours</u>. This means that things are kept <u>secret</u>. A good example of this is when Elizabeth <u>lies</u> about John's <u>affair</u> out of fear that his <u>reputation</u> will be ruined if she tells the truth.

Puritans are expected to live by the <u>strict rules</u> of society if they want to be part of a <u>community</u>. But they also want to be <u>individuals</u>, so they sometimes <u>break the rules</u>. People are encouraged to <u>report</u> anyone who breaks the rules, because that person is thought to be putting <u>society</u> at <u>risk</u> by offending God.

Fear of being <u>cast out</u> works at a <u>smaller scale</u> too — Mary Warren breaks down and takes back her claim that the girls are lying when she realises she'll be forced out of her <u>social group</u>.

2) People like Sarah Good and Goody Osburn, who <u>don't conform</u> to what's expected, aren't seen as part of the community. For such a close-knit community, who live under threat of <u>attack</u> by Native Americans (see p.7), being cast out like this is a <u>terrible fate</u>.

3) The witchcraft accusations start because the girls have been caught dancing in the forest — they're too <u>scared</u> to <u>tell the truth</u> about what they were doing, so it gets blown <u>out of proportion</u>.

Fear quickly develops into hysteria

1) The "hundred or more" <u>confessions</u> are taken as <u>proof</u> that witches are "gathered in monstrous attack" on Salem. People are <u>scared</u> of being <u>bewitched</u> or <u>accused</u> of witchcraft and the town becomes <u>hysterical</u>.

2) <u>Evidence</u> for witchcraft is based on <u>hearsay</u>, e.g. Goody Putnam says Betty was <u>seen flying</u> "over Ingersoll's barn". Like <u>Chinese whispers</u>, rumours get changed and make people more <u>scared and hysterical</u>.

3) Mary Warren's behaviour in Act Three shows how the <u>power of suggestion</u> can feed hysteria. The other girls insist that they see a yellow bird, which <u>convinces</u> her that she does too, until she's "<u>screaming madly</u>".

 KEY QUOTE *"There is prodigious danger in the seeking of loose spirits."*
Unlike most people in Salem, Rebecca Nurse (a.k.a. 'the voice of reason') isn't scared of witchcraft, but she is worried about how destructive rumours and fear can be. It's a shame no-one listens to her...

Identity and Reputation

For the people of Salem, a name is a bit more than just something your mates yell to get your attention. It's all about what other people think of you — and more importantly what you think of yourself.

Reputations are easily damaged

The characters fall into two groups — those who want to improve their reputation (e.g. Abigail, Parris) and those who want to protect their reputation (e.g. Proctor and the judges).

1) In Act One, Abigail's <u>angry</u> that other villagers are <u>spreading rumours</u> about her.

2) She hasn't found another <u>job</u> after being <u>fired</u> by the Proctors — this shows how much <u>importance</u> the villagers place on <u>reputation</u>.

<u>Parris</u> worries that if people find out that he <u>can't control</u> his own niece's actions, they'll think he shouldn't hold a position of <u>power</u> in Salem.

3) When Parris finds out that the girls <u>conjured spirits</u>, his first concern is his <u>job</u> and <u>reputation</u> — he says "They will topple me with this!"

Elizabeth says that there's "a certain <u>danger</u>" in accusing someone who has a <u>good reputation</u> — if an accusation <u>isn't believed</u>, it would cast <u>doubt</u> on the other accusations, and therefore on the <u>girls' motives</u>.

4) Once the trials begin, Abigail's reputation <u>changes</u> to the point where she's a "<u>saint</u>", and she can <u>destroy</u> a person's reputation just by <u>mentioning their name</u>.

Some characters identify themselves by their moral values

1) Some characters have a better developed sense of <u>right and wrong</u> than others — their <u>identity</u> is strongly linked to their <u>conscience</u>.

2) These characters <u>won't go against their moral values</u> and confess to something they haven't done — like Rebecca Nurse and Elizabeth Proctor. This allows them to retain their <u>identity</u>.

3) For Proctor, his <u>name</u> comes to <u>represent his reputation</u>, and by confessing he feels he's betraying who he is. His <u>sense of identity changes</u> throughout the play:

© AJ Chan

- He's aware how <u>important</u> his <u>name</u> is from the start — he tells Putnam "We vote by name in this society, not by acreage." This suggests a person's name gives them <u>power</u> and <u>rights</u>.

- He <u>puts off</u> testifying against Abigail in case people find out about the affair and his <u>name</u> is <u>ruined</u>.

- He realises that he has to <u>risk his reputation</u> to save his friends, so he <u>admits</u> to the affair.

- He's in <u>conflict</u> over his own <u>identity</u> — "God in Heaven, what is John Proctor, what is John Proctor?" He's not worried about signing a <u>false confession</u>, because he is "no saint".

- He sees that <u>lying</u> to save his own life goes against everything he wants to be, and that he can't <u>live</u> without his <u>identity</u> — "I have given you my soul; leave me my name!"

- He <u>rips up</u> his confession and dies feeling <u>happy</u> with <u>who he is</u>.

KEY QUOTE

"I have rung the doom of my good name"

Proctor's reputation is so important to him that when he finally owns up to his affair with Abigail, it's like suffering a death in the family. The "bell" of his honour is like a funeral bell ringing for the loss of his name.

Loyalty

It might seem as though everyone in Salem is pretty keen to betray everyone else to get themselves out of trouble. However, there are a few shining examples of people being loyal to one another.

The Proctors are loyal to each other despite their problems

1) Proctor has an affair with Abigail, which isn't very loyal, but he <u>ends it</u> and <u>confesses</u> to Elizabeth.

2) He feels very <u>guilty</u> about being unfaithful, and he shows his <u>loyalty to Elizabeth</u> in other ways too:

- He gets <u>angry</u> with Abigail when she <u>insults</u> Elizabeth.

- He <u>sacrifices</u> his reputation to save Elizabeth — "My wife is innocent, except she knew a whore when she saw one!"

- He <u>defends</u> her against the <u>accusations</u> of witchcraft, <u>tearing up</u> the warrant for her arrest, <u>threatening</u> Cheever and Herrick, and <u>promising</u> to "fall like an ocean" on the court.

Proctor's loyal to the other characters too — e.g. he refuses to accuse anyone else of witchcraft when he confesses.

3) Elizabeth also shows <u>absolute loyalty</u> to Proctor throughout the play — in particular when she <u>lies</u> about his affair for the sake of his <u>reputation</u>, even though she's <u>committing a sin</u> by doing so.

© AJ Chan

Some of the other characters are loyal too. E.g. <u>Giles Corey</u> won't say who told him Putnam was "reaching out for land" because if he does they'll be <u>arrested</u>. He's prepared to face <u>arrest himself</u> rather than <u>betray</u> a friend.

Other characters are loyal to their jobs or beliefs

1) Some characters show a <u>misplaced loyalty</u> to the <u>court</u> and <u>authority</u> — for example, <u>Cheever</u> seems to feel <u>no doubt</u> or <u>shame</u> at arresting people he's known all his life.

2) <u>Danforth</u> and <u>Hathorne</u> are the only major characters who remain <u>completely loyal</u> to the <u>court</u> throughout — their refusal to see the truth of the accusations makes them seem <u>arrogant</u> and <u>narrow-minded</u>.

3) Hale's loyalties <u>change</u> as the play progresses:

Historical Background

Proctor has <u>flaws</u> but he's a <u>heroic figure</u> throughout because he's <u>decent</u> and <u>loyal</u>. This shows us that Miller <u>admires</u> those people who stayed <u>loyal</u> during <u>McCarthyism</u>.

- In Act One he's <u>convinced</u> that he will <u>expose</u> any witches in Salem. He's loyal to <u>authority</u> and the <u>pursuit of knowledge</u> — he's certain that his books let him understand "all the invisible world".

- In Act Two he <u>admits</u> to John Proctor that he has <u>wondered</u> whether people are only confessing to <u>save their own lives</u>, but he still <u>believes</u> in "the justice of the court".

- By Act Three he sees that his loyalty to the court is <u>misplaced</u>, and tries to defend those accused. He finally <u>walks out</u> in protest — "I denounce these proceedings, I quit this court!"

- In Act Four he has <u>shifted</u> his loyalty to the <u>prisoners</u> — he tries to persuade Danforth to <u>release</u> them.

EXAM TIP

Use evidence from the text to support your argument...

It doesn't matter how good your argument is — if it's not supported with evidence, the examiner won't be happy. Just saying that Elizabeth is loyal won't cut it — use a quote to show how you know that.

Practice Questions

Phew, another section under your belt. This one is probably the trickiest so far, so make sure you understand the different themes in 'The Crucible' by answering these questions...

Quick Questions

1) Why are the girls scared to admit that they were dancing in the forest?

2) What is rumoured to have happened to the court in Andover?

3) How does Parris try to discredit John Proctor in court?

4) Why do the Putnams want to get revenge on Rebecca Nurse?

5) Why did some people think that getting rid of witches would make their lives better?

6) Why doesn't Parris want to admit that the girls were practising witchcraft?

7) What reputation does Abigail have in Salem at the start of the play?

8) Find a quote that shows how important John's sense of identity is to him.

9) Give one example of a point in the play where one character is loyal to another.

10) Who or what are the judges loyal to?

Practice Questions

Examiners love marking questions about themes, so you need to be prepared to write something marvellous in the exam. These in-depth questions should help you get your head round things, and the exam-style questions are a handy taster of the kind of thing you might get, yep, you guessed it... in the exam. Mmm, delicious.

In-depth Questions

1) What do you think are the main emotions that drive Reverend Parris's actions? Explain your answer.

2) How does John Proctor's sense of identity change over the course of the play?

3) Which character do you think best represents the theme of loyalty? Explain your answer.

4) Do you think Abigail's desire for revenge is the main cause of the events of *The Crucible*? Explain your answer.

5) What part do you think religious intolerance plays in driving the events of the play?

Exam-style Questions

1) How does Miller present ideas about conscience and loyalty in *The Crucible*?

2) How effective is Act One in introducing the themes presented in *The Crucible*?

3) 'The events of *The Crucible* are driven solely by fear.' To what extent do you agree with this statement?

4) How does Miller present ideas about identity in *The Crucible*?

How 'The Crucible' Looks On Stage

It's really important to remember that *The Crucible* is a play, so it's meant to be watched. This means you've got to think about the stage directions, lighting, costumes etc. as well as what the characters say.

The setting is important

The Crucible has <u>four acts</u>. Each act takes place in a <u>single location</u>. And each location tells the audience something about the characters and events <u>associated</u> with it.

Act One — Betty Parris's bedroom

1) The "*clean spareness*" of Betty's room reflects the Puritans' <u>simple</u> way of life.

2) "*A candle still burns*" next to Betty's bed, which could symbolise <u>hope</u>. Miller says in the stage directions that the Puritans still believed they carried "*the candle that would light the world.*"

Act Two — Proctor's common room

1) The Proctors' house is a bit like their <u>marriage</u>. It's a "*long*" room which allows John and Elizabeth to keep their <u>distance</u> from each other, both <u>physically</u> and <u>emotionally</u>. It's "*dark*" too — the darkness keeps things <u>hidden</u>, just like they hide their <u>feelings</u> from each other.

2) But there's a fireplace — this signifies underlying <u>warmth</u> and that there's <u>hope</u> for the relationship.

Act Three — The meeting house

1) The meeting house doubles up as a <u>church</u> and a <u>court</u>.

2) Traditionally, churches offer people <u>hope</u> and <u>sanctuary</u>, so it's ironic that in *The Crucible* people are <u>condemned</u> there.

Act Four — The jail

1) The jail is a symbol of Salem's <u>repression</u>. There's "*a high barred window*" and "*heavy door*" making escape seem impossible.

2) At first, the jail appears empty, but the "*bundle of rags*" lying on a bench turns out to be Sarah Good. The conditions are <u>appalling</u> and <u>inhumane</u>.

Miller isn't specific about the characters' costumes

The stage directions don't say what the costumes should look like but most productions of the play choose to dress the characters in a <u>similar way</u>:

1) The girls are dressed <u>alike</u> — to show how they aren't seen as <u>individuals</u>.

2) The judges are usually in <u>black</u> and <u>white</u>. This reflects how they see the world in terms of <u>good</u> and <u>evil</u> with nothing in between.

3) The <u>down-to-earth</u> farmers like Proctor and Corey often wear earthy colours, like <u>browns</u> and <u>greens</u>.

4) Sarah Good and the other prisoners wear <u>rags</u> to show their <u>suffering</u>.

5) Proctor is described as carrying a <u>gun</u> several times — this is a symbol of his <u>dominance</u> and <u>masculinity</u>.

© AJ Chan

Learn about what each setting symbolises...

Make sure you can remember what each setting in the play symbolises. Analysing the whole play rather than just the dialogue will show the examiner that you really understand what Miller was trying to say.

The Structure of 'The Crucible'

Structure. If a play doesn't have it, there'll be no tension. No tension, no drama. No drama, no audience. No audience, no good. Oh, and if your essay doesn't have structure... Yep, you've guessed it. No marks.

The Crucible is a tragedy

1) A <u>tragedy</u> is a story which ends with the <u>suffering</u> or <u>death</u> of the main character. Their death has usually been caused by a <u>flaw</u> in their personality.

2) In *The Crucible*, John Proctor is a classic <u>tragic hero</u>. He ends up <u>dead</u> because he <u>lusts</u> after Abigail — his <u>affair</u> with her sparks off the witch trials which lead to his <u>downfall</u>.

3) The story is made more tragic because Proctor is a <u>likable</u> character — he's <u>brave</u>, he has <u>strong morals</u> and despite his affair he <u>loves</u> his wife.

4) Miller made John Proctor an '<u>everyman</u>'. He <u>isn't perfect</u> — the audience can <u>identify</u> and <u>empathise</u> with his <u>struggles</u>.

An everyman is a typical, ordinary person

5) But by the end of the play he's <u>changed</u>. He can see a "shred of goodness" in himself — he's learned to <u>forgive</u> himself for his faults.

Some characters don't change

1) The <u>change</u> in Proctor's character <u>contrasts</u> with those characters who don't learn <u>anything</u> from the witch trials.

2) At the start of the play, Parris is <u>selfish</u> — he's only concerned with his <u>reputation</u>. By the end he hasn't changed — he wants to <u>postpone</u> the hangings to <u>protect</u> himself from riots rather than to <u>save</u> Proctor.

3) Throughout the play Danforth is driven largely by his desire to protect his <u>reputation</u>. In Act Three he's <u>proud</u> of the fact that he's "<u>condemned</u> to hang" seventy-two people for witchcraft. In Act Four he seems to realise the prisoners are <u>innocent</u>, but he <u>refuses to pardon</u> them because it "speaks a <u>floundering</u>" on his part.

© AJ Chan

4) Abigail is <u>remorseless</u> from start to finish — she tries to <u>destroy</u> the Proctors' marriage, tries to get <u>revenge</u> on the women of Salem by sending them to their <u>deaths</u> and never feels any <u>guilt</u> about her actions.

Exits and entrances develop the plot

The coming and goings of the characters on stage are <u>significant</u>. They:

- <u>reveal</u> things about characters. In Act One, Tituba exits the stage with Parris shouting at her. She's clearly <u>defenceless</u> and an <u>easy scapegoat</u> for Abigail's accusations.

- <u>create drama</u>. In Act Three, when Elizabeth is asked whether Proctor's telling the truth about his affair with Abigail, her entrance is <u>carefully staged</u> — she doesn't come face-to-face with Abigail. The two characters never <u>communicate</u> directly, which <u>increases</u> the feeling of <u>tension</u> and <u>dislike</u> between them.

- <u>signal a change</u>. In Act Two Hale arrives at the Proctors' house <u>alone</u> — this shows he's acting <u>without</u> the court's authority and thinks the trials may be going <u>too far</u>.

The Structure of 'The Crucible'

Creating tension and making the action well-paced is pretty important to playwrights.
Too many thrills and your audience gets saturated with action, too few and they're dozing off in the aisles.

The pace of the play is relentless

© 20TH CENTURY FOX / THE KOBAL COLLECTION / WETCHER, BARRY

1) There aren't any scene changes within acts to interrupt the audience's attention.

2) There isn't really any comedy to lighten the atmosphere.

3) Miller lengthens the amount of time that passes between scenes. Between Acts One and Two a week has passed, but three months has gone by between Acts Three and Four. This gives a feeling of doom — things haven't improved even after a fairly long period of time.

4) The fast pace means there isn't enough time to think things over — people act rashly and things quickly spiral out of control.

Each act has its own internal structure

1) All four acts start with a tense scene that creates a sense of expectancy but they all end in high drama.

Act One starts with Parris quietly praying by his daughter's bed. It's tense — we don't know if she's dead or alive.	Act One ends with Tituba, Abigail and Betty making hysterical accusations against innocent people.
Act Two opens with John and Elizabeth trying to please each other. It's tense — neither of them gets it quite right.	Act Two ends with Proctor violently grabbing Mary Warren by the throat and throwing her to the floor.
Act Three starts with an empty room. The first voices are offstage, so we're not entirely sure what's happening.	Act Three ends with Proctor laughing insanely and Hale quitting the court and slamming the door.
Act Four starts with an apparently empty room, but the heap of rags turns out to be Sarah Good quietly sleeping.	Act Four ends with John going to his death.

2) The contrast between the suspense of the opening, and the emotion of the climax means the audience aren't numbed by constant drama in each act.

3) Each act slowly builds up the tension and keeps the audience on the edge of their seats — they know that the hysteria could break out at any time.

EXAM TIP

Write about how the structure of the play affects the audience...

Make sure you understand how Miller shaped the structure of the play to have an impact on the audience.
For example, you could write about how the intensity of the dramatic events keeps the audience engrossed.

Language in 'The Crucible'

It ain't what you say, it's the way that you say it. Some people can tell a joke, for instance, and have everyone in hysterics. Whilst other people… can't. Which reminds me, did you hear the one about the…

Miller uses old-fashioned English to set the scene

1) Miller uses old-fashioned language to try and represent how people would have talked 300 years ago. He does this by:

   - using old words such as "Goody" (short for Goodwife) and "gulling" (to trick or fool)
   - making the grammar sound unusual e.g. "What think you, Mr. Parris?"

2) This type of language makes the dialogue sound more realistic and reminds the audience that the play's based on real events — this helps the audience to empathise with the characters.

3) He doesn't overdo it though because it might be difficult for a modern audience to understand. He just tries to give the impression that the language is old.

He also uses biblical language and Latin

© AJ Chan

1) The characters often make reference to the Bible e.g. "Do you know your Commandments?" This shows how much religion was part of their daily life.

2) Characters such as Elizabeth Proctor and Rebecca Nurse use biblical language and refer to God frequently — e.g. Elizabeth says that wherever Abigail goes "the crowd will part like the sea for Israel." It's ironic that the characters who are condemned for witchcraft are shown to be the most Christian and God-fearing.

3) Hale and Danforth occasionally use Latin. This makes them seem more educated and means that the other characters can't understand them, which increases their power.

The less educated characters have their own speech patterns

1) The less educated characters have more rural sounding speech patterns e.g.:

   - double negatives, e.g. Tituba says, "I don't compact with no Devil"
   - they drop the final "g" in words such as "searchin'" and "whippin'"
   - coarse language — Proctor tells the court they are "raising up a whore"

2) This kind of speech makes the characters more believable — the audience can identify with them.

3) It also creates a contrast with the upper-class speech of the men in authority. This shows the power divide in Salem — characters with power such as Hale and Danforth are never accused of witchcraft but the less educated characters like Tituba and John Proctor are easy targets.

Language in 'The Crucible'

The way we speak says a lot about the kind of people we are — so it's really important in a play to give each character a distinctive way of speaking that reflects their personality.

Proctor and Abigail use powerful language

Proctor isn't afraid to speak his mind e.g. he tells Hale "You are a broken minister" when Hale arrests his wife. His language is consistent — he's an honest, steady character.

1) Proctor speaks straight from the heart and is very direct, e.g. he calls Abigail a "whore".

2) He's sarcastic — he tells Parris, "you spoke so long on deeds and mortgages I thought it were an auction".

3) Proctor has a poetic way of speaking at times e.g. he uses similes "fall like an ocean", metaphors, "an everlasting funeral marches round your heart" and personification, "vengeance is walking Salem".

4) Abigail also uses poetic language such as the simile "sweated like a stallion".

5) Abigail's language is inconsistent — she adapts how she talks depending on who she's speaking to. She flirts with Proctor, she threatens the girls, and she's easily offended when anyone accuses her of anything.

Abigail's ability to adapt her language shows us she's smart, but it also shows how easily she can manipulate people.

Other characters also have distinctive ways of speaking

1) Elizabeth speaks simply, but what she says shows that she's wise, e.g. "Do what you will. But let none be your judge."

2) Danforth uses hyperbole to show how powerful he is, e.g. he would "hang ten thousand that dared to rise against the law".

Hyperbole is the technical term for when a writer exaggerates something.

3) Hale's language changes during the play. At the start he's confident — "Have no fear now" — but towards the end the audience can sense his guilt when he says "I come to do the Devil's work."

Miller uses language to control the pace of the play

1) In Act One, the quick-fire questioning of Tituba panics her into confessing. It doesn't give her time to think.

2) In Act Two, the tense, stilted conversation between Proctor and Elizabeth slows the pace and creates discomfort.

3) In Act Three, when all the girls start screaming together, it creates a sense of hysteria.

4) In Act Four, the accused seem resigned to their fate and their speech is calmer to reflect this. Elizabeth speaks "quietly" and "gently" with Hale and Proctor.

© 20thC.Fox/Everett/Rex Features

KEY QUOTE

"They be tellin' lies about my wife"

When Giles Corey pleads with Danforth, his simple, rural language contrasts with Danforth's complicated, upper-class speech. Miller uses this contrast to highlight Corey's weakness and Danforth's power.

Imagery and Symbolism in 'The Crucible'

Imagery and symbolism in *The Crucible* is a bit tricky to get your head round. But examiners love it when you write about this sort of stuff, so make sure you know it inside out.

Miller makes lots of references to light

1) In Acts One and Three <u>sunlight</u> shines on the stage. Usually when light shines on something we see it more <u>clearly</u> — in these scenes the sunshine highlights the <u>deceit</u>.

For more on <u>stage lighting</u> have a look at page 50.

2) The description of Abigail shrouded in a *"pearly light"* is <u>ironic</u>. Pearly light suggests <u>angels</u> and <u>heaven</u>, and she's far from angelic.

3) Proctor says he sees "no <u>light</u> of God" in Parris — he doesn't think Parris is a <u>genuine</u> Christian.

4) In the end, as Proctor and Rebecca are taken away to be hanged, the *"new sun"* pours onto Elizabeth's face — this symbolises <u>change</u> dawning on Salem. Miller states that "the power of theocracy... was <u>broken</u>" by the witch trials.

The cold is used to symbolise a lack of human feeling

1) Abigail tells Proctor, "You are no <u>wintry</u> man". She knows that he isn't <u>cold</u> — he's <u>passionate</u>.

2) Tituba says that the Devil "<u>freeze</u> his soul in Massachusetts," while in Barbados he "be singin' and dancin'". She thinks the <u>cold</u>, <u>repressed</u> residents of Salem "riles him up" and make him cruel and <u>unfeeling</u>.

3) Mary describes the "misty <u>coldness</u>" that comes over her in court. It's as if human warmth has <u>left</u> her.

4) Elizabeth says she kept a "<u>cold</u> house" — she uses the house as a <u>metaphor</u> for the fact that she's <u>emotionally cold</u> and unable to <u>express</u> her feelings <u>properly</u>.

Heat and fire symbolise passion — but also the Devil

1) The Puritans saw sex outside of marriage as very <u>sinful</u>.

2) The devil is also associated with <u>heat</u> — sinners' souls are believed to <u>burn</u> in hell.

3) Abigail says "I have a sense for heat, John" and she describes him "burning" in his loneliness. This represents Abigail's <u>passion</u> but also the heat of their <u>sin</u>.

4) In Act Four, Danforth says of the trials "We burn a hot fire here; it melts down all concealment". This makes the audience think about the similarities between the <u>court</u> and <u>hell</u>.

© 20thC.Fox/Everett/Rex Features

Danforth's words also link the court to the idea of a crucible — see p.49.

Imagery and Symbolism in 'The Crucible'

The Puritans weren't into symbols, they took the Bible literally, and thought its teachings were directly relevant to their lives. If only they'd seen witches as symbols of fun or kittens then things may have turned out better.

A crucible is a symbol of purification

1) A crucible is a <u>container</u> that can be heated to high temperatures — it's used to separate the <u>pure</u> bits of metal from the <u>not so pure</u> bits.

2) The witch trials are the 'crucible' that purify Salem of <u>hypocrisy</u> and <u>theocracy</u>.

3) A crucible can also be a <u>test</u> to judge the <u>quality</u> and <u>strength</u> of something. In the play, many characters are tested by the witch trials, and their quality and strength is <u>revealed</u> — for example, the prisoners who <u>refuse</u> to confess reveal their <u>courage</u> and <u>integrity</u>.

4) The trials also purify some of the characters, like Proctor who sees a "shred of goodness" in himself at the end of the play — he's been <u>cleansed</u> of his sins.

5) Elizabeth and John's relationship is severely <u>tested</u>, but the trials make their relationship <u>stronger</u> because they have learned to be <u>honest</u> with themselves and each other.

> Ultimately the <u>corrupt</u> society <u>purifies</u> itself. "Echoes Down the Corridor" tells us that the power of <u>theocracy</u> is finally <u>destroyed</u>.

Birds represent people's spirits

1) In Act Three, the girls pretend to see Mary Warren's <u>spirit</u> in the form of a <u>yellow bird</u>.

2) When Sarah Good sees herself and Tituba as a "pair of bluebirds wingin' southerly", it reminds us that the Puritans fled England to <u>avoid</u> persecution, but are now <u>causing</u> other people to <u>flee</u>.

3) In Act Four, Herrick describes Proctor as sitting "like some great bird". It's as if his <u>soul</u> has returned to him now he's <u>confessed</u> to his affair with Abigail.

The law is represented as a heavy burden

1) Hale describes his books as "<u>weighted</u> with authority".

2) Giles Corey is <u>crushed</u> to death by heavy stones. The stones represent the <u>weight of the law</u> that says his sons won't inherit if he enters a plea.

3) When Elizabeth is arrested, she is bound by <u>heavy</u> chains.

4) Cheever remarks "how heavy" the <u>law</u> is, and how he has to carry its "<u>tonnage</u>" on his back.

> Miller's representation of the law as a burden emphasises the <u>struggle</u> the characters face between following <u>society's rules</u> or following their own <u>conscience</u>.

© Felicity Peacock

 "the light of God is in him"

Hale thinks that "light" represents goodness, which is usually true. However, here it's a sign that, although Hale thinks something is true, the audience can see he's wrong — Parris isn't actually a very good person.

Stage Directions in 'The Crucible'

Don't be fooled into thinking that *The Crucible* is just a sort of drama documentary of exactly what happened in Salem. Miller has adapted and shaped the characters and events to make the story work well on stage.

Miller gives background information in his stage directions

Miller wrote mini-essays explaining the <u>historical context</u> and giving <u>introductory profiles</u> for some of the characters. These sections aren't usually performed but they do have several functions:

- They remind the reader that the play was based on <u>real events</u>.

- These sections mean the play can be <u>read</u> as well as <u>performed</u>. The extra information helps readers see what <u>motivates</u> the characters and actors to <u>imagine</u> how they would play a <u>particular part</u>.

- They show that Miller had a very <u>clear</u> idea of how the play should look on the stage — the lengthy stage directions don't give much <u>flexibility</u> to directors.

Stage directions reveal a lot about the characters

A lot of the events in the play are <u>caused</u> by the way characters <u>feel</u>. Stage directions tell the actors what kind of <u>tone of voice</u> and <u>body language</u> to use to make these feelings <u>clear</u>.

© Felicity Peacock

1) In Act One when Parris says, "No - no" with "*his eyes going wide*" we know he is <u>alarmed</u>, not just disagreeing.

2) When Abigail approaches Proctor "*Winningly*" in Act One she does it "*with a confidential, wicked air*". This shows that she is a <u>seductive</u> character.

3) Elizabeth is described as "*blushing with pleasure*" when Proctor compliments her cooking in Act Two — it's clear she's trying to <u>please</u> him.

The stage directions say the lighting should be natural

1) Miller gives clear <u>instructions</u> on how the stage should be <u>lit</u>.

| <u>Act One</u> opens with "*morning sunlight*" | ➔ | <u>Act Three</u> has "*sunlight*" pouring on to the stage. | ➔ | <u>Act Four</u> has "*moonlight seeping through the bars*" | ➔ | At the end of <u>Act Four</u> "*new sun*" falls on Elizabeth's face |

2) The lighting mimics <u>natural</u> light — this contrasts with the <u>unnatural</u> accusations.

3) The natural light also reminds the audience that people are being accused in the <u>cold light of day</u>, not under the cover of <u>darkness</u>. There's no attempt to <u>hide</u> the trials and <u>nowhere</u> for the accused to hide. For more on light as a symbol see p.48.

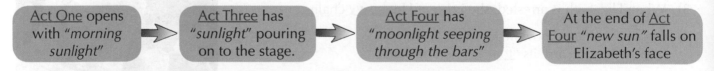

EXAM TIP

Never underestimate the importance of stage directions...

Stage directions may only make up a small part of the play, but that doesn't mean you should ignore them. You can usually make a few points about them in any answer, so try to learn this stuff really well.

Practice Questions

Here are some quick questions to warm you up. Keep practising until you can do them in your sleep.
Although be careful that reciting answers in your sleep doesn't get you accused of witchcraft...

Quick Questions

1) What does the *"clean spareness"* of Betty's room in Act One tell you about the Puritans?

2) Why might a director choose to dress the young girls alike?

3) Miller gives clear instructions in the stage directions on the type of light to be used.
   Should it be: a) natural b) fluorescent c) flashing?

4) Give two reasons why entrances and exits in *The Crucible* are important.

5) Which characters sometimes speak in Latin?

6) Give two features of the speech patterns used by less educated characters in *The Crucible*.

7) List three words which describe Proctor's language.

8) Which characters tend to use a lot of religious language?

9) Why is the *"pearly light"* which surrounds Abigail in Act One ironic?

10) List three important symbols Miller uses in *The Crucible*.

Practice Questions

My advice on tackling this page? Try to answer the in-depth questions first. If they're easy-peasy then move on to a couple of the exam-style questions for a bit more of a challenge. If, however, the in-depth questions prove a wee bit tricky, get a drink of tea/juice/water and a biscuit (the biscuit is vital for success) and read the chapter again. I know it's booooooring but it's the best way to learn.

In-depth Questions

1) Why do you think Miller uses mini-essays to give historical background in *The Crucible*?

2) Give two examples of tragic events that happen in *The Crucible*, and say why they're tragic.

3) How does Miller use the girls' language in Act Three to build hysteria?

4) Why is each of the different settings in the play important?

Exam-style Questions

1) What is the significance of the title of *The Crucible*?

2) Choose a passage from the play that you find especially tense. What methods does Miller use to create tension and suspense in the passage?

3) Write about the ways Miller uses language in *The Crucible* to make his characters seem believable.

Exam Preparation

Getting to know the text will put you at a massive advantage in the exam. It's not enough just to read it though — you've got to get to grips with the nitty-gritty bits. It's all about gathering evidence...

The exam questions will test three main skills

You will need to show the examiner that you can:

1) Write about the play in a thoughtful way — picking out appropriate examples and quotations to back up your opinions.

2) Identify and explain features of the play's form, structure and language. Show how Miller uses these to present the ideas, themes, characters and settings effectively.

3) Write in a clear, well-structured way. 5% of the marks in your English Literature exams are for spelling, punctuation and grammar. Make sure that your writing is as accurate as possible.

Preparation is important

1) It's important to cover all the different sections of this book in your revision. You need to make sure you understand the text's context, plot, characters, themes and writer's techniques.

2) In the exam, you'll need to bring together your ideas about these topics to answer the question quickly.

3) Think about the different characters and themes in the text, and write down some key points and ideas about each one. Then, find some evidence to support each point — this could be something from any of the sections in this book. You could set out your evidence in a table like this:

Theme: Religion	
Puritanism and theocracy	Puritans strict Christians. Society based on religion — Church powerful. "The law, based upon the Bible". Court believes it's guided by God.
Belief in the Devil	People really believe in the Devil — "who came to you with the Devil?" See the world in terms of conflict between God and the Devil.
Intolerance	Anyone who doesn't conform seen as a threat — suspected of being influenced by the Devil, e.g. Tituba. Fear of otherness.
Opposition to intolerance	Proctor sees importance of individual freedom all along. Witch trials show Hale dangers of intolerance.
Biblical language	Characters often refer to Bible — religion part of everyday life. "Remember what the angel Raphael saint".

Preparing to succeed — a cunning plot indeed...

Knowing the plot inside out will be unbelievably helpful in the exam. It'll help you to stay calm and make sure you write a brilliant answer that positively glitters with little gems of evidence. The exam's just a chance for you to show off...

The Exam Question

This page deals with how to approach an exam question. The stuff below will help you get started on a scorching exam answer, more scorching than, say, a phoenix cooking fiery fajitas in a flaming furnace.

Read the question carefully and underline key words

1) The style of question you'll get depends on which <u>exam board</u> you're taking.

2) Read all the <u>instructions</u> carefully. Make sure you know <u>how many</u> questions you need to answer and <u>how much time</u> you should spend answering each one.

3) If the question has <u>more than one part</u>, look at the total number of marks for each bit. This should help you to plan your <u>time</u> in the exam.

4) <u>Read</u> the question at least <u>twice</u> so you completely understand it. <u>Underline</u> the key words. If you're given an <u>extract</u>, underline <u>important</u> words or phrases in that too.

Henry didn't read the weather report carefully enough when planning his weekend activities.

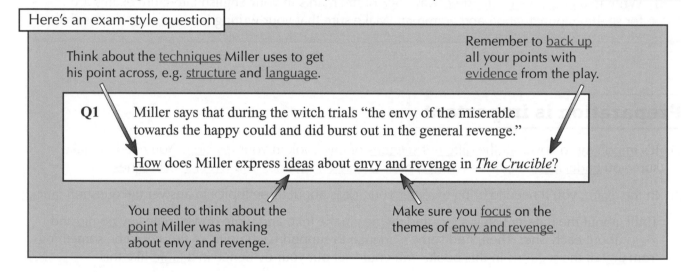

Here's an exam-style question

Think about the <u>techniques</u> Miller uses to get his point across, e.g. <u>structure</u> and <u>language</u>.

Remember to <u>back up</u> all your points with <u>evidence</u> from the play.

Q1 Miller says that during the witch trials "the envy of the miserable towards the happy could and did burst out in the general revenge."

<u>How</u> does Miller express <u>ideas</u> about <u>envy and revenge</u> in *The Crucible*?

You need to think about the <u>point</u> Miller was making about envy and revenge.

Make sure you <u>focus</u> on the themes of <u>envy and revenge</u>.

Get to know exam language

Some <u>words</u> come up time and again in <u>exam questions</u>. Have a look at some <u>specimen</u> questions, pick out words that are <u>often used</u> in questions and make sure that you <u>understand</u> what they mean. You could <u>write a few down</u> whilst you're revising. For example:

Question Word	You need to...
Explore / Explain	Show <u>how</u> the writer deals with a <u>theme</u>, <u>character</u> or <u>idea</u>. Make several <u>different</u> points to answer the question.
How does	Think about the <u>techniques</u> or <u>literary features</u> that the author uses to get their point across.
Give examples	Use <u>direct quotes</u> and describe <u>events</u> from the text in your own words.
Refer to	Read the question so that you know if you need to write about just an <u>extract</u>, or an extract and the <u>rest of the text</u>.

The advice squad — the best cops in the NYPD...

Whatever question you're asked in the exam, your answer should touch on the main characters, themes, structure and language of the text. All the stuff we've covered in the rest of the book in fact. It's so neat, it's almost like we planned it.

Planning Your Answer

I'll say this once — and then I'll probably repeat it several times — it is absolutely, completely, totally and utterly essential that you make a plan before you start writing. Only a fool jumps right in without a plan...

Plan your answer before you start

1) If you plan, you're less likely to forget something <u>important</u>.

2) A good plan will help you <u>organise</u> your ideas — and write a good, <u>well-structured</u> essay.

3) Write your plan at the <u>top of your answer booklet</u> and draw a <u>neat line</u> through it when you've finished.

4) <u>Don't</u> spend <u>too long</u> on your plan. It's only <u>rough work</u>, so you don't need to write in full sentences. Here are a few <u>examples</u> of different ways you can plan your answer:

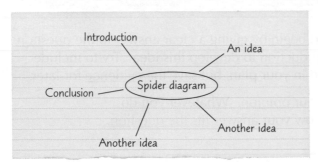

Bullet points...
- Introduction...
- An idea...
- The next idea...
- Another idea...
- Yet another idea...
- Conclusion...

Include bits of evidence in your plan

1) <u>Writing</u> your essay will be much <u>easier</u> if you include <u>important quotes</u> and <u>examples</u> in your plan.

2) You could include them in a <u>table</u> like this one:

3) <u>Don't</u> spend <u>too long</u> writing out quotes though. It's just to make sure you <u>don't forget</u> anything when you write your answer.

A point...	Quote to back this up...
Another point...	Quote...
A different point...	Example...
A brand new point...	Quote...

Structure your answer

| Introduction |
| ↓ |
| Middle Section |
| — paragraphs |
| expanding |
| your |
| argument. |
| ↓ |
| Conclusion |

1) Your <u>introduction</u> should give a brief answer to the question you're writing about. Make it clear how you're going to <u>tackle the topic</u>.

2) The <u>middle section</u> of your essay should explain your answer in detail and give evidence to back it up. Write a <u>paragraph</u> for each point you make. Make sure you <u>comment</u> on your evidence and <u>explain how</u> it helps to <u>prove</u> your point.

3) Remember to write a <u>conclusion</u> — a paragraph at the end which <u>sums up</u> your <u>main points</u>. There's <u>more</u> about introductions and conclusions on the <u>next page</u>.

Dirk finally felt ready to tackle the topic.

To plan or not to plan, that is the question...

The answer is yes, yes, a thousand times yes. Often students dive right in, worried that planning will take up valuable time. But 5 minutes spent organising a well-structured answer is loads better than pages of waffle. Mmm waffles.

Writing Introductions and Conclusions

Now you've made that plan that I was banging on about on the last page, you'll know what your main points are. This is going to make writing your introduction and conclusion as easy as pie.

Get to the point straight away in your introduction

1) First, you need to work out what the question is asking you to do:

> **How is the character of John Hale important to the play?**
>
> The question is asking you to think about the role of John Hale in the text.
> Plan your essay by thinking about how this character links to the text's overall message.

2) When you've planned your essay, you should begin by giving a clear answer to the question in a sentence or two. Use the rest of the introduction to develop this idea. Try to include the main paragraph ideas that you have listed in your plan, but save the evidence for later.

3) You could also use the introduction to give your opinion. Whatever you do, make sure your introduction makes it clear how your answer fits the question.

Your conclusion must answer the question

1) The most important thing you have to do at the end of your writing is to summarise your answer to the question.

2) It's your last chance to persuade the examiner, so make your main point again.

3) Use your last sentence to really impress the examiner — it will make your essay stand out. You could develop your own opinion of the text or highlight which of your points you thought was the most interesting.

The examiner was struggling to see the answer clearly.

Use the question words in your introduction and conclusion

1) Try to use words or phrases from the question in your introduction and conclusion.

> **How does Miller use stage directions in the play?**

2) This will show the examiner that you're answering the question.

> Miller uses stage directions in 'The Crucible' to explain the historical context of the play, to introduce some characters and to show how the characters feel.

The first sentence of the introduction gives a clear answer, which will lead on to the rest of the essay.

3) This will also help you keep the question fresh in your mind so your answer doesn't wander off-topic.

I've come to the conclusion that I really like pie...

To conclude, the introduction eases the examiner in gently, whilst the conclusion is your last chance to impress. But remember — the examiner doesn't want to see any new points lurking in those closing sentences.

Writing Main Paragraphs

So we've covered the beginning and the end, now it's time for the meaty bit. The roast beef in between the prawn cocktail and the treacle tart. This page is about how to structure your paragraphs. It's quite simple...

P.E.E.D. is how to put your argument together

Remember to start a new paragraph every time you make a new point.

1) P.E.E.D. stands for: Point, Example, Explain, Develop.

2) Begin each paragraph by making a point. Then give an example from the text (either a quote or a description). Next, explain how your example backs up your point.

3) Finally, try to develop your point by writing about its effect on the reader, how it links to another part of the text or what the writer's intention is in including it.

Use short quotes to support your ideas

1) Don't just use words from the play to show what happens in the plot...

> Parris thinks that people are plotting against him — he says to Abigail "my enemies ... will ruin me".

This just gives an example from the text without offering any explanation or analysis.

2) Instead, it's much better to use short quotes as evidence to support a point you're making.

3) It makes the essay structure clearer and smoother if most quotes are embedded in your sentences.

It's better to use short, embedded quotes as evidence. Then you can go on to explain them.

> When Betty falls ill, Parris seems more worried about what his "enemies" will think than he is about his daughter. This shows Parris's obsession with his reputation, and the strength of his paranoia about people plotting against him.

Get to know some literary language

1) Using literary terms in your answer will make your essay stand out — as long as you use them correctly.

2) When you're revising, think about literary terms that are relevant to the text and how you might include them in an essay. Take a look at the table below for some examples.

Literary Term	Definition	Example
Metaphor	Describing something by saying it is something else.	"This farm's a continent when you go foot by foot"
Dramatic Irony	When the audience knows something that a character doesn't.	"I am sure they may have nothing to fear."
Epilogue	A scene or speech at the end of a play, which often tells you about the characters' fates.	The epilogue in *The Crucible* reveals that the witch trials broke theocracy's power in Salem.

This page is so exciting — I nearly...

Now now, let's all be grown-ups and avoid the obvious joke. It's a good way of remembering how to structure your paragraphs though. Point, Example, Explain, Develop. Simple. Maybe we could make a rap or something... anyone?

In the Exam

Keeping cool in the exam can be tricky. But if you take in all the stuff on this page, you'll soon have it down to a fine art. Then you can stroll out of that exam hall with the swagger of an essay-writing master.

Don't panic if you make a mistake

1) Okay, so say you've timed the exam beautifully. Instead of putting your feet up on the desk for the last 5 minutes, it's a good idea to <u>read through</u> your <u>answers</u> and <u>correct any mistakes</u>...

2) If you want to get rid of a mistake, <u>cross it out</u>. <u>Don't scribble</u> it out as this can look messy. Make any corrections <u>neatly</u> and <u>clearly</u> instead of writing on top of the words you've already written.

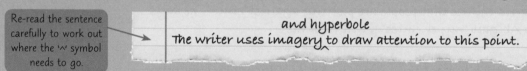

The author uses various literary ~~teknikues~~ techniques to explore this theme .

> This is the clearest way to correct a mistake. Don't be tempted to try writing on top of the original word.

3) If you've <u>left out</u> a <u>word</u> or a <u>phrase</u> and you've got space to add it in <u>above</u> the line it's missing from, write the missing bit above the line with a '∧' to show exactly where it should go.

> Re-read the sentence carefully to work out where the '∧' symbol needs to go.

The writer uses imagery ∧ to draw attention to this point.
and hyperbole

4) If you've left out whole <u>sentences</u> or <u>paragraphs</u>, write them in a <u>separate section</u> at the <u>end</u> of the essay. Put a <u>star</u> (*) next to both the <u>extra writing</u> and the <u>place</u> you want it to go.

Always keep an eye on the time

1) It's surprisingly <u>easy</u> to <u>run out of time</u> in exams. You've got to leave <u>enough time</u> to answer <u>all</u> the questions you're asked to do. You've also got to leave enough time to <u>finish</u> each essay properly — with a <u>clear ending</u>.

2) Here are some <u>tips</u> on how to <u>avoid</u> running out of time:

- Work out <u>how much time</u> you have for each part of your answer <u>before</u> you <u>start</u>.
- Take off a few minutes at the beginning to <u>plan</u>, and a <u>few minutes</u> at the end for your <u>conclusion</u>.
- Make sure you have a <u>watch</u> to <u>time yourself</u> — and keep checking it.
- Be <u>strict</u> with yourself — if you spend <u>too long</u> on one part of your answer, you may run out of time.
- If you're <u>running out of time</u>, keep <u>calm</u>, <u>finish</u> the <u>point</u> you're on and move on to your <u>conclusion</u>.

Stephanie never had a problem with keeping cool.

Treat an exam like a spa day — just relax...

Some people actually do lose the plot when they get into the exam. The trick is to keep calm and well... carry on. If you make sure you get your exam technique sorted, you'll be as relaxed as a sloth in a room full of easy chairs.

Sample Exam Question

And now the bit you've all been waiting for — a sample exam question and a lovely little plan.
Go make yourself a cup of tea, settle down and enjoy.

Here's a sample exam question

Read this feisty exam question. That's the best way to start...

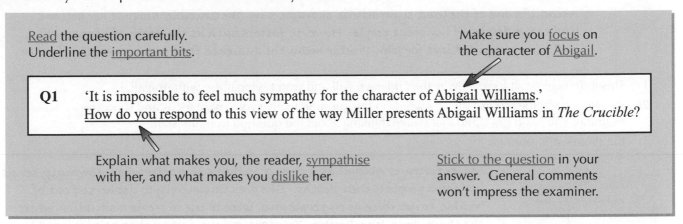

Read the question carefully.
Underline the important bits.

Make sure you focus on
the character of Abigail.

Q1 'It is impossible to feel much sympathy for the character of Abigail Williams.'
How do you respond to this view of the way Miller presents Abigail Williams in *The Crucible*?

Explain what makes you, the reader, sympathise
with her, and what makes you dislike her.

Stick to the question in your
answer. General comments
won't impress the examiner.

Here's how you could plan your answer...

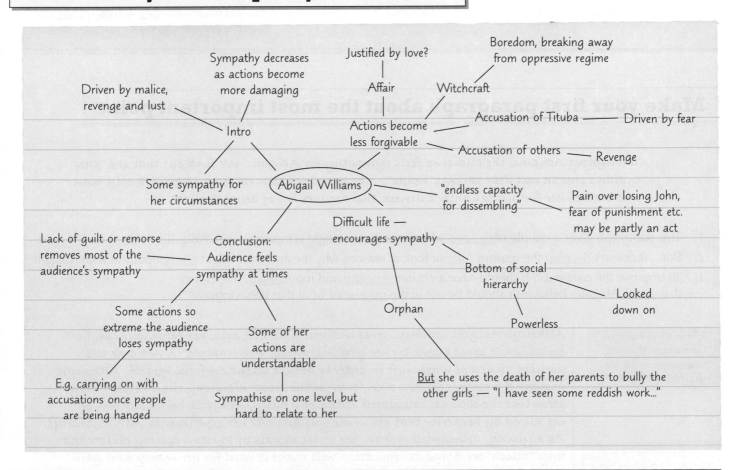

Boredom, breaking away
from oppressive regime

Sympathy decreases
as actions become
more damaging

Justified by love?

Driven by malice,
revenge and lust

Affair   Witchcraft

Intro

Actions become
less forgivable

Accusation of Tituba ——— Driven by fear

Accusation of others ——— Revenge

Some sympathy for
her circumstances

Abigail Williams

"endless capacity
for dissembling"

Pain over losing John,
fear of punishment etc.
may be partly an act

Lack of guilt or remorse
removes most of the
audience's sympathy

Conclusion:
Audience feels
sympathy at times

Difficult life —
encourages sympathy

Bottom of social
hierarchy

Looked
down on

Orphan

Powerless

Some actions so
extreme the audience
loses sympathy

Some of her
actions are
understandable

But she uses the death of her parents to bully the
other girls — "I have seen some reddish work..."

E.g. carrying on with
accusations once people
are being hanged

Sympathise on one level, but
hard to relate to her

What do examiners eat? Why, egg-sam-wiches of course...

The most important thing to remember is DON'T PANIC. Take a deep breath, read the questions, pick a good 'un, write
a plan... take another deep breath... and start writing. Leave five minutes at the end to check your answer too.

Worked Answer

These pages will show you how to take an okay answer and turn it into a really good one that will impress the examiner.

Use your introduction to get off to a good start

These pages are all about how to word your sentences to impress the examiner, so we haven't included everything from the plan on page 59.

You might start with something like...

> Abigail is one of the least sympathetic characters in 'The Crucible' because her actions lead to the deaths of innocent people. However, factors such as the death of her parents and her unrequited love for John Proctor mean the audience feels some sympathy for her.

1) This intro is <u>okay</u>. It looks at why the audience will and won't sympathise with Abigail.

2) It's also a good idea to use the <u>key words</u> in the question to give your essay <u>focus</u> and show the examiner you're on <u>track</u> and that you're thinking about the question from the start.

3) But there's still room for <u>improvement</u>...

This shows that you're focused not just on the audience's reaction to Abigail, but on how Miller intended her to come across.

> Miller portrays Abigail as a strong, ruthless character who knowingly sends innocent people to their deaths. She does this merely to get herself out of trouble, to get revenge on people and, later, to try to create a situation where she can marry John Proctor. There are various factors that go some way to explaining her behaviour, so the extent to which the audience sympathises with her depends on the extent to which they view her increasingly malicious actions as understandable in the context of her background.

This tells the examiner what the essay's about and shows that you've thought about your essay structure.

Make your first paragraph about the most important point

> Throughout Act One, the audience feels sympathy for Abigail. We find out that she "saw Indians smash my dear parents' heads". She has since been raised by Parris, a cold man who blames her for his daughter's illness and accuses her of being "soiled".

1) This paragraph gives a couple of <u>reasons</u> why the audience might sympathise with Abigail.

2) But... it doesn't <u>develop</u> the reasons <u>fully</u> or look at reasons why the audience might <u>not</u> sympathise with Abigail.

3) To improve the paragraph it should have a clearer <u>structure</u> and more <u>detail</u>. The points that <u>justify</u> Abigail's behaviour should be put in the <u>context</u> of what that behaviour <u>is</u>.

This is a well-balanced introduction that tells the examiner what the paragraph will be about.

Offering alternative points of view shows you've really thought about your answer.

> Although Abigail commits some indisputably evil acts, her behaviour can be explained to some extent by her circumstances. For example, in Act One she accuses Tituba of witchcraft in order to deflect attention from herself. Although accusing a slave, someone even lower in the social hierarchy than herself, may seem like the callous, calculated action of a bully, Abigail's behaviour can be explained by her terror that her uncle will discover her experiments with witchcraft. As a young, unmarried orphan, the strict morals of Puritan society dictate that any "blush" on Abigail's reputation will make it hard for her marry and gain any independence. Miller therefore encourages the audience to feel a degree of sympathy for her during the early scenes of the play.

Referring back to the question keeps your answer focused.

Worked Answer

You need to make a variety of points

After you've explained why the audience might sympathise with Abigail, you could start your next point like this:

> The audience's sympathy for Abigail ends when she accuses Elizabeth Proctor — her only motives at this point are lust for John Proctor and revenge.

1) It introduces the idea that Abigail's actions become more extreme and less forgivable.

2) However, you can make this paragraph better by giving more detailed examples and backing up points with quotes.

Linking words show you're changing topics and makes the structure clearer.

> However, as the play progresses it becomes clear that Abigail is prepared to kill innocent people in order to satisfy her own lust, envy and desire for revenge, so the audience's sympathy for her is largely lost. A good example of this is when she accuses Elizabeth of witchcraft for the "monstrous profit" of becoming John's wife once Elizabeth is hanged. The word "monstrous" emphasises how evil and unnatural Abigail is.

Analysing specific words and phrases will impress the examiner.

3) You could also develop it by considering how real the audience believes Abigail's pain and love are:

> Miller describes Abigail as having "an endless capacity for dissembling", and her acting ability is seen through the way she uses language and body language to manipulate people, e.g. "[quavering, as she sits]: I would never hurt Betty." The audience quickly comes to distrust her, so that even speeches that would normally provoke sympathy, e.g. "John, pity me, pity me!" cause the audience to question how genuine her distress is.

Mentioning stage directions shows you're aware that The Crucible is a play and that you've thought about more than just what the character says.

Finish your essay in style

You could say:

> In conclusion, the audience feels some sympathy for Abigail at times, because she has had a difficult life. However, many of her actions cannot be justified by her circumstances, so overall the audience feels little sympathy for her.

1) This conclusion is okay but it doesn't summarise how Miller makes the reader feel a certain way about Abigail.

2) So to make it really impressive you could say something like...

> At the start of the play, the audience feels some sympathy for Abigail, as she is trapped in a difficult situation and feels compelled to resort to desperate measures to avoid punishment. However, her capacity for lying and manipulating others soon becomes evident, for example through her shift from "apprehension and propriety" with Parris to her threats and bullying of the other girls in Act One. This causes the audience to distrust Abigail and question her real motives. By the end of the play, it is clear that Abigail is driven by a desire for revenge and power, and feels no remorse for the lives she has taken, so she emerges as a wholly unsympathetic character.

This focuses on the question. The word "However" shows that you're thinking about both sides of the argument.

Make your last sentence really stand out — it's your last opportunity to impress the examiner.

Why do alligators write good essays? Their quotes are so snappy...

It seems like there's a lot to remember on these two pages, but there's not really. To summarise — write a good intro and conclusion, make a good range of points (one per paragraph) and put your most important point in paragraph one. Easy.

Index

Arthur Miller's The Crucible

The Characters from 'The Crucible'

Phew! You should be an expert on *The Crucible* by now. But if you want a bit of light relief and a quick recap of the play's plot, sit yourself down and read through *The Crucible — The Cartoon*...

John Proctor

In jail

Elizabeth Proctor

In jail

Abigail Williams

Reverend Parris

Reverend Hale

Thomas and Ann Putnam

Giles Corey

Tituba

Mary Warren

Deputy-Governor Danforth

Rebecca Nurse

In jail

Arthur Miller's 'The Crucible'

ETC42